D1266653

REVELATION

REVELATION

by

GUSTAF AULÉN
KARL BARTH
SERGIUS BULGAKOFF
M. C. D'ARCY
T. S. ELIOT
WALTER M. HORTON
WILLIAM TEMPLE

edited by
JOHN BAILLIE
and
HUGH MARTIN

FABER AND FABER LIMITED
24 Russell Square
London

First published in June Mcmxxxvii
by Faber and Faber Limited
24 Russell Square London W.C. 1
Printed in Great Britain by
R. MacLehose and Company Limited
The University Press Glasgow

CONTENTS

vii

Contents

PREFACE

Among the more hopeful signs of the time is the appearance of the various oecumenical or world movements that now unite the various branches of the Christian Church. Chief of these are the World Conference on Faith and Order, the Universal Christian Council on Life and Work, and the International Missionary Council. Each is at the present time looking forward, after a decade of elaborate and careful preparation, to an important conference —the first-mentioned at Edinburgh in August 1937, the second at Oxford in July 1937, the last at Hangchow, China, in September-October 1938.

The modest volume now offered to the public may be said to have grown out of the preparations that are being made for all three of these conferences; for all three movements have been, in one informal way or another, connected with the proposal which has led to its compilation. A discussion of the nature and limits and content of revelation must in the first instance fall within the scope of the Church's *faith and order*, and it is in this connection that the present discussion has been primarily undertaken. Yet as an ever greater concentration of thought has been devoted to the problems

b

R.

of the Church's *life and work* in our own time, the more have these problems been felt to 'remount', as they say in French, to the problem of revelation. It is at this point that the conflict becomes most acute between the distinctively Christian attitude to life and that attitude of secularistic humanism which so largely dominates the modern scene. When again we pass to the issues that are at present confronting the *missionary enterprise* of the Church, we find increasingly the same thing to be true. More and more the missionary problem is becoming a theological problem. More and more are our missionaries concerned with the clarification of the content of their message—a clarification that has been forced on them particularly by the rapid eastward spread of our western mechanistic and secularised culture, as well as by the heightened self-consciousness of some of the eastern religious cults.

It would appear then that the topic of revelation is of the first order of urgency as regards the Church's total task in the present age. Ample evidence of a widespread recognition of this fact may be found in the degree of attention which theologians of all lands and communions are at present devoting to the subject. Indeed if one were asked what was, just at the present moment, the most frequented hunting ground of the theologians, one would have to answer without hesitation that it was

the doctrine of revelation—a sufficiently remarkable contrast to the situation obtaining in, say, the years immediately prior to the Great War. This little book, emerging as it does out of this contemporary discussion, is intended as a contribution towards the task and witness of the Church militant in the present age. It is an attempt on the part of the Christian mind of our time to assert and vindicate its faith in the light of the total existing situation.

Unfortunately, however, the Christian mind of our time is in many respects a divided mind; and there can be no denying that there is serious division in respect of this doctrine of revelation. There is also, it need hardly be said, a large and important area of agreement. At the very least there seems to be agreement as to the vital nature of the question. And *that there is revelation* is something which all parties seem equally concerned to proclaim. But there is undoubtedly also a very large measure of agreement as to what the revelation is. Mr. Eliot writes in his contribution: 'The division between those who accept, and those who deny, Christian revelation, I take to be the most profound division between human beings.' All the contributors to this book stand emphatically and irrevocably on the same side of this dividing line, and to that extent the book may be taken as a Christian manifesto addressed to the world at large. But for the rest, and to a not inconsiderable extent, the reader is rather invited to overhear a discussion that is being carried on openly in his presence. We have not made the least effort to conceal the wide divergences of view which exist among Christian thinkers in this field; on the contrary, it has been our aim to bring these divergences into relief. For it has been our conviction that this problem is little likely to be solved by those who are unwilling to face the plain facts of the situation in a realistic way. Among these facts are the deep differences that divide communion from communion and confession from confession. Even more serious in our own day would seem to be the horizontal differences that cut across these vertical ones—the new divergences that divide, not so much the denominations, as the schools of interpretation. What hope is there of ever transcending such differences, if we do not first make it our business clearly to understand their nature and clearly to define their extent?

What we have done, therefore, has been to invite seven distinguished writers representing different Christian traditions—different communions as well as divergent schools of thought—to explain to us their own understanding of the meaning of revelation in the light of the various traditions in which they stand. Bishop Aulén was invited as a fitting representative of Lutheranism and Scandinavia. Dr. Barth, representing the Swiss Church of the Reformation, was invited to set forth the view which he has made so peculiarly his own and which has deeply influenced Christian thought in so many different communions. The Russian Dr. Bulgakoff was invited from the Orthodox Church because he is generally recognized to be one of the most eminent thinkers of that Church. To represent the Roman Catholic Church Father D'Arcy was invited, as one who, in addition to being in a position of trust within his own communion, has won the ear of the British public in a somewhat remarkable way. Professor Horton, who is a Baptist, was singled out as an eminent and typical representative of the rising generation of Christian thinkers in America. It will be agreed that to represent the Church of England, and indeed our British theological thought in general, nobody could have been found more suitable than the Archbishop of York. Finally, the task of writing an introductory essay of a more general kind was pressed upon Mr. T. S. Eliot as one who, standing on the frontier between theology and *belles-lettres*, has of late years done so much to interpret literature to the theologian and theology to the man of letters. With great kindness all these agreed to the proposal. Each contributed an essay, the essays were then circulated among the contributors, and each was given the opportunity to revise his own essay in the light of what the others had written. The result now lies before the reader.

Preface

The idea of revelation has from the beginning played an all-important part in the thought of the Christian Church. From the very first it was taught and believed that the saving knowledge of God in Christ which the Church exists to proclaim was a knowledge which had come to man only by way of a definite act and activity of self-disclosure on the part of God Himself. But from a very early period this revealed knowledge of God was set in contrast to another kind of knowledge which was called natural or rational. It was taught that while some truths about God could be found out by man himself, there were other truths, and those most vital to salvation, which man could never come to know, if they had not been communicated to him by God through the medium of Holy Writ. The classic position accepted in the Middle Ages was that reason is able to inform us *that God is* and *what He is not*; that this negative knowledge of His nature may be eked out by what was called the Method of Analogy so as to include positive affirmation of His unity, His infinity and His goodness; but that the doctrine of the Holy Trinity, and with it all the specifically *Christian* teaching about God and about the way of salvation He has provided in Christ His Son, must always remain a matter of *faith*, to be accepted on the authority of God's revealed Word alone.

The first leaders of the Protestant Reformation

tended, though in varying degrees, to disturb this mediaeval settlement by restricting the sphere of rational discovery and minimizing its importance, but in the Protestantism of succeeding generations and centuries this particular deviation from Catholic teaching was much less remarkable, even where it did not altogether disappear. However, in the growing humanism and rationalism of the seventeenth and eighteenth centuries an opposite tendency soon began to declare itself—the tendency to place ever greater weight upon rational discovery and *either* to be sceptical as to whether any revelation had actually been granted at all *or* to insist that such revelation did not add anything essential to what was rationally discoverable but was merely a gracious 'republication' of rational truth to a world that was otherwise in danger of missing it, or of losing it after it had once been possessed.

On the whole, the eighteenth century embraced the latter of these two alternatives. But the nineteenth century seemed often to prefer the former. During that latter period it grew to be more and more the habit, not only among academic philosophers, but to a considerable extent also among theologians and religious thinkers generally, to speak of our Christian knowledge in terms of human discovery, and to make less and less use of the terminology of revelation. Our religion was thus in serious danger of coming to be regarded as something spun by ourselves out of our own substance, and no longer as God's gracious provision to enlighten our darkness and minister to our sore need.

Against this tendency the twentieth century has already witnessed a remarkable reaction. This reaction may, up to the present, have manifested itself only within limited circles, but these limited circles would seem to be precisely the places in which the thought of the future is being prepared. Not only post-War theology, not only many schools of post-War philosophy, but also many movements in the general literature—and even in the art—of our time bear witness to the prevailing revolt against the humanistic outlook, and especially against the necessarily *subjectivistic* orientation of that outlook, which had so long dominated the thought, and therefore the life, of the West. Anthropocentrism has, to say the least, suffered a severe setback; and there is a growing disposition to believe once again that our religion, if we are to have one at all, must be something given to us by God rather than provided by ourselves. Manifestations of this new awakening will be found almost everywhere throughout this volume.

The question may, however, be raised whether this involves a return to the *status quo ante*. Were humanism and rationalism mere aberrations? Have we nothing to learn from the deistic protest, from the *Aufklärung*, from romanticism, from nine-teenth-century liberalism? Shall we go back to the old doctrine of revelation, or shall we seek a new and better one? It is here that there is still sharp division of opinion, and the reader will soon discover that such division is represented in this book. There are those who, while wholeheartedly believing that only by a gracious act of self-disclosure on the part of God Himself could we ever come to possess the saving knowledge of Him which is ours in Christ, would yet hold that in the older tradition this divine self-disclosure was wrongly understood as a mere communication—sometimes even as a dictation—of information, and was therefore set in false antithesis with the human activity of the intellectual and spiritual quest for Him. Such would hold that there is no proper antithesis between thinking on the one hand and the reception of revelation on the other, any more than there is between intelligent reflection concerning one's duty and divine guidance concerning it; and they would accordingly insist that the protest of humanism and liberalism against the idea of revelation, in spite of all the disastrous lengths to which it was carried (until at last it threatened altogether to destroy our religious heritage), had yet a necessary mission to fulfil in the clarification of our thought. It was, they would say, the confused traditional conception of the nature of revelation that was largely responsible for its rejection by so many men of obvious good will. This view will be found represented in the pages that follow; but an opposite view will also be found there—the view of those who still believe the old antithesis of reason and revelation to be an essentially correct one, and who see no hope of our returning to a right way of thinking on these matters until we resolutely turn our backs upon humanism with all its works. These would submit that all so-called modern re-explanations of the idea of revelation will turn out in the end to be only so many attempts to explain it away.

The question is further complicated by the growing tendency to substitute for the old distinction of natural and revealed knowledge of God the new distinction between a general and a special revelation. This changed way of regarding the matter was sometimes hinted at by the older writers who pointed out that there was a sense in which even natural knowledge could be spoken of as revelation—an *internal* revelation, as the Reformer Zwingli called it in his *De Vera et Falsa Religione* (1525); but the full development of the usage would appear to be modern. It will be seen at once that the old and apparently so clear distinction between natural and revealed knowledge is in this way traversed and superseded; and that not because the revealed knowledge is naturalized but

Preface

because the natural knowledge is now drawn up into the sphere of revelation. It is now asserted that God has revealed Himself, His mind and His will, not only in Christ and the Scriptures, but to some extent also in the pre-Christian and non-Christian religious traditions of the world, in the ordinary processes of thought, in philosophy, in external nature, in human history; though only in Christ and the Scriptures are we put in possession of the special revelation of His saving grace. Towards the issues thus raised the contributors to the present volume will be found very variously disposed. Professor Barth, if I rightly understand him, would hold that only in Christ have we any true knowledge of God at all; there is no natural knowledge of God, and only in 'a perverted, invalid and loose sense' of the concept can there be said to exist any revelation apart from Christ. Father D'Arcy very valiantly defends the distinction between natural and revealed (or supernatural) knowledge, showing himself equally anxious to give the former its due measure of recognition and to exhibit the very restricted limits within which it must always continue to move. Though differing from Dr. Barth regarding the existence of a natural knowledge of God, he agrees with him in holding that only in a loose sense can it be allowed that there is revelation outside of the Christian proclamation. Professor Bulgakoff, on the other hand, insists that every one of the pagan religions 'contains a kernel of divine revelation', and also that 'there exists a natural revelation of God in His creation, in nature, and in the human spirit'. Bishop Aulén has much to say of general revelation—of that rather than of natural knowledge—but is at the same time acutely aware of the risks involved in the conception. Two dangers, he writes, threaten theology—'one is the isolation of the revelation of God in Christ; another is the use of the "general" revelation in a way that leads to a deification of man or of human ordinances'. The Archbishop of York contends that 'in all creation some revelation of God is offered' (though it may be that only in a small measure is it effectually received), and likewise that there is a real revelation of God in each of the positive religions; yet it is upon the inadequacy of such revelations that he too lays his emphasis. Mr. Eliot wishes to 'take for granted that Christian revelation is the only full revelation; and that the fullness of the Christian revelation resides in the essential fact of the Incarnation'. And indeed there is nothing that seems to be more insisted on by all the writers than the close connection between revelation and incarnation. The Word, we are reminded again and again, was revealed *by being made flesh*. Professor Horton, finally, wishes to retain both the conception of natural (or rational) knowledge and the conception of general revelation, giving separate meaning to each, and allowing the relative right of both, while again reserving his emphasis for the ultimately hopeless inability of either to meet our real need. I hope I have not done injustice to any of the writers in this brief comparison of their deliverances upon a point on which many will be anxious to consult them. My desire is only to refer readers to the essays themselves.

Perhaps the complex nature of the problem may be brought out in another way. We are all agreed that there is no hope of deliverance from the evils that are threatening our age, and that so often appear to be leading us to the abyss of dissolution, save in the wholehearted reassertion, as over against the prevailing secularism of our age, of the revelation of God in Christ. And yet it may be doubted whether the word 'secularism' expresses quite the whole truth about the world's temper in the present decade. Perhaps secularism is beginning to give way to something even more disquieting—to something which instead of being merely human is actually *demonic*. Perhaps the struggle of Christianity in the next age will not be so much against religionlessness as against false and evil religions. The new philosophies of life that are springing up in many countries in close alliance with certain political programmes are hardly any longer to be characterized as secularist. They are no longer rationalistic, but violently opposed to rationalism; flouting at reason rather than appealing to it overmuch. They are violently anti-liberal. They are not libertarian, but strongly authoritarian, despising freedom of thought and speech and action, and exalting obedience. In their perverse way, therefore, they too must be regarded as belonging to the temper of the new age rather than to that of the old one; taking the form rather of pretended *counter revelations*, preached with fanatical and almost messianic fervour by leaders who, far from relying on the *lumen siccum* of a bygone Age of Reason, are rather as men possessed. Such being the situation, our Christian task is obviously not completed when we have led men back to a new realization of the necessity of revelation. There is a sense in which the new age seems very ready to be convinced. We may yet see the spectacle of competing 'revelations' attempting to shout one another down, all alike refusing to submit themselves to any standard of judgment but their own. A large part of our task must therefore lie in the clarification of our grounds for embracing, and pleading with others to embrace, the proffered *Christian* revelation in preference to all such pretended rivals.

It will be realized, then, how deeply the discussions here engaged in enter into the practical predicament of the present age, and how far they are from being merely academic in their interest. The writers have, indeed, immersed themselves in the complexities of the subject itself, sometimes with little explicit reference to the larger theatre of action in which their debate is being conducted; yet there is hardly a page in which they do not betray to the understanding reader their profound sense of the solemnity and urgency of the issue in which they are all the time engaged.

A heavy share of the detailed work involved in the undertaking has been borne by my co-editor, the Rev. Hugh Martin of the Student Christian Movement Press. My own share was to have been undertaken by my dear friend and honoured teacher and colleague, the late Professor H. R. Mackintosh, and it was only after his lamented death, and when the work was already well in hand, that I was called upon to take his place. Dr. Barth's contribution has been translated by the Rev. J. O. Cobham, Principal, and the Rev. R. J. C Gutteridge, Tutor, of the Queen's College, Edgbaston, Birmingham. Dr. Bulgakoff's contribution has been translated by the Rev. Oliver F. Clarke and Miss Xenia Braikevitch, Editors of *Sobornost*. In the correction of the proofs we have had the valuable help of the Rev. J. Y. Campbell, formerly of Yale University and now of Kilmacolm, Scotland. To each of these are due our cordial thanks. Finally, however, we would express a very special measure of gratitude

Preface

to Dr. J. H. Oldham, who has been unsparing with his help and advice, and to whom the book owes more than it would be easy to express.

JOHN BAILLIE

The University of Edinburgh,
April 1937

I

By T. S. ELIOT

What I have to write is not an introduction
to the essays in this book, but an introduction to
the subject; and it is because I am not a theologian
that I have been asked to contribute. I am not to
concern myself with the different forms in which
men may hold a doctrine of revelation, or with the
consequences they may deduce from it; either
with the different theological systems, nor with
the different Christian communions. I am concerned with the general differences between those
who maintain a doctrine of revelation and those
who reject all revelation. I am assumed to have an
intimate and affectionate acquaintance with the
limbo and lower regions in which the secular
world moves: a knowledge of objects towards
which the theological mind is not often directed.
My qualification is the eye of the owl, not that of
the eagle.

I take for granted that Christian revelation is

A   I   R.

the only full revelation; and that the fullness of Christian revelation resides in the essential fact of the Incarnation, in relation to which all Christian revelation is to be understood.

The division between those who accept, and those who deny, Christian revelation I take to be the most profound division between human beings. It does not merely go deeper than divisions by political faith, divisions of class or race; it is different in kind, and cannot be measured by the same scale. It need not cancel these divisions, in so far as they represent principles of union and not of discord. To deny the ties of blood and of congeniality wholly would be to widen the chasm between the Church and the World, and obstruct our indirect, still more than our direct, missionary activity. The emphasis should be on what binds together Christians the world over, rather than on what divides them from others: so that Christian brotherhood should be not merely an idea held, a phrase spoken, but something consistently felt. Nevertheless, it is well for us to study what I may call the folk-lore and practices of the non-Christian world, for we shall not convert it unless we understand it.

The line to be drawn between the Christian and the non-Christian world is at present extremely difficult to draw. It is not enough, for our present purposes, to propound the wholesome reflexion that not all those who deny Christ are necessarily His enemies, and that many who profess Him are living by the World. The first remark to be made is that not even the *Oxford English Dictionary* definition of secularism is quite comprehensive:

'The doctrine that morality should be based solely on regard to the well-being of mankind in the present life, to the exclusion of all considerations drawn from belief in God or in a future state.'

A doctrine of morality based not *solely*, but *primarily*, on regard to the well-being of mankind in the present life might also be classified as secularist. Also, what escapes the necessary concision of a dictionary definition, notions of what the 'present life' is, and accordingly of what 'well-being' is, may vary extremely; and we can only say that secularism *tends* to restrict the conception to what we call, still vaguely, 'material' well-being. And finally, a belief may be far from excluding considerations drawn from belief in God or in a future state, and yet, because of its conception of the nature of God, or of the future state, still be predominantly secularist.

The first error would be to identify secularism with what was called rationalism. I say 'what was called', because the word 'rationalism' can in general mean so much that in particular it is likely to mean something very much less, and

to have accidental associations. The rationalism
of the nineteenth century (that of the Rationalist
Press Society) now seems very old-fashioned:
the rationalism of Tyndall, Haeckel, and Mr.
Bernard Shaw. This antiquation is not the result of any religious revival but, I believe, of
a further stage of religious decay. In countries
like France where Christianity still means for
the most part the Roman Catholic Church, and
means a traditional Catholicism rather than one
of individual conversion, the *non*-Christian forces
are still *anti*-Christian, and therefore maintain
a repudiation of anything that might be associated with religion. The sceptical state of
mind is there still fundamentally Cartesian; and
in spite of the appearance of Bergson—whose
mind does not seem to me characteristically
French—I am inclined to believe that philosophies which admit the inclusion of the irrational,
or of anything which eludes rational grasp—such
as *vitalism*—are more natural to non-'Latin'
countries where the decay of Christianity has
followed a different route. The English rationalism
of the nineteenth century—not only that of the
popular scientists but that of literary folk like
George Eliot and Leslie Stephen—had more in
common with Latin rationalism of today; though
there was in it a rigid Puritan zeal, a confidence
that the disappearance of Christianity would

coincide with enlightenment and progress, which strikes us as not only obsolete but provincial.

In the English-speaking world of today, the rationalist is no longer quite so rationalistic. The change is partly, and evidently, due to further scientific discovery, and the growth of popular belief that no particular scientific theory can be accepted more than provisionally. One may cite such situations as that in which it is necessary for a physicist to hold two contradictory theories at once in order to be able to deal with different phenomena. A greater meekness is observed, and even a rush of scientists to stake out a little quasi-religious territory for themselves.

The formation of the Fabian Society in the latter years of the nineteenth century brought a bubbling-up to the intellectual surface of society of able men of imperfectly developed sensibilities. The kind of philosophy of life which Mr. Shaw and Mr. H. G. Wells had to offer no doubt seemed to them satisfactory for all because it was satisfactory to themselves. If you are so fortunate (from the point of view of this world) as to have no immortal longings, and are furthermore gifted with such fluency in writing as to be kept perpetually entertained by your own talents, you can be easily satisfied. But in some more recent writers we find a more defensive tone: they are anxious to assure their readers that the future, in a world in which science will replace religion, is *not* going to be dreary. The most readable of contemporary popular writers on science is Mr. Gerald Heard. The epilogue to his *Science in the Making* contains the following remarkable statement:

'Man, who has left to appetite the task of finding for him the worth of living, of being the sole sauce with which to give him the gusto to bite off and digest great chunks of the stubborn outer world, will find appetite sated almost before it can stir. Humanity will be bored. The mysterious word which first stole like a grey shadow over the court of *le Roi Soleil*, and then spread to all places where men of taste lived beyond the struggle for meats and mates, will percolate down from class to class till all are leisured, all are idly rich with a wealth of time on their hands, no people have ever possessed, ever been embarrassed with, before. If then mankind is not too weary of its life, to fly to making intentionally the accidents, the strains and anxieties which gave it thrills and spurs and sudden convictions that life is worth while (but which nature no longer makes for it) if it is not, through war, deliberately to break down into anarchy the order it has built up, it must find new interest and excitement. There is only one appetite from which this new stock of interest can spring and that is curiosity, the finest of the passions. Curiosity is impersonal and so can

6

remain when all personal appetites have been paid off. Curiosity is not utilitarian and so can carry on when men are sated with means. Curiosity is inexhaustible and so can find fresh fields and new explorations when all the world that man can exploit is ordered, every sight has been seen and every power exercised.'

I have said that this statement is remarkable. Readers will be reminded, by the turgid style rather than by the ill-constructed sentences, of that remarkable effusion of twenty years ago, Mr. Bertrand Russell's *Free Man's Worship*. There is a considerable difference; there is twenty years' difference. Mr. Heard's affirmation is still more incredible than Mr. Russell's. *Curiosity the finest of the passions!* Vanity of vanities!

Another writer for whom I have considerable respect, Mr. Herbert Read, has made a still more recent statement for himself which might be taken as an amendment, rather than a contradiction of Mr. Heard's:

'Just as curiosity is the faculty which drives man to seek out the hidden structure of the external universe, thereby enabling him to build up that body of knowledge which we call Science, so wonder is the faculty which dares man to create what has not before existed, which dares man to use his powers in new ways and for new effects. We have lost this sense of the word

7

"wonderful"—it is one of the most outworn clichés in the language. But actually "wonder" is a better and more inclusive word than "beauty", and what is full of wonder has the most compelling force over the imagination of men.'

I adduce these quotations as evidence that the more reflective writers of this generation—those whose attention is not wholly taken up by prospective political and social reforms, and who therefore have the time to consider final ends—feel the need for assuring us that mankind still has something to live for. As the pleasures of iconoclasm subside, most of the idols having been demolished or removed to museums, the iconoclasts find it necessary to look about for objects to supply the needs that the idols satisfied. The result of offering an *activity*, such as 'curiosity' or 'wonder', to replace an *end*, is to make that activity appear a great deal more petty and trifling than it is to the person with religious faith. Curiosity or wonder, being exalted above its proper place, becomes a tedious activity, for it becomes merely a restless search for more sensation (it is not worthy of the name of experience) of the same kind. One would have thought that Aristotle had said everything there was to be said on such matters, if the kinds of doctrine that Aristotle refuted had not flourished rather more luxuriantly after his time than before. A sound ethical doctrine is frequently replaced neither by one that is sounder, nor by one that is antithetical to it, but by one or more each of which selects some element of it to the exclusion of others.

A writer who is chronologically half-way between Shaw on the one hand and Heard and Read on the other, Mr. Bertrand Russell, wrote a book called *The Conquest of Happiness*, which may be called a defence of mediocrity. It comes to the conclusion that so far as happiness depends upon oneself, and not upon circumstances, 'the recipe for happiness is a very simple one'. It is simple, of course, because Mr. Russell simplified the problem to the degree of falsification. I do not propose to analyse his argument, in which is incorporated a great deal of advice, based partly upon the discovery by modern psychology of things that were known already, that is quite commonplace and perfectly acceptable. And he sometimes imagines that he is controverting traditional views when he is merely stating them in a partial way. For instance, he says:

'Professional moralists (*he does not say which*) have made too much of self-denial, and in so doing have put the emphasis in the wrong place. Conscious self-denial leaves a man self-absorbed and vividly aware of what he has sacrificed; in consequence it fails often of its immediate object and almost always of its ultimate purpose. What is needed is not self-denial, but that kind of direction of interest outward which will lead spontaneously and naturally to the same acts that a person absorbed in the pursuit of his own virtue could only perform by means of conscious self-denial.'

The passage is interesting as a specimen of the confusion of thought into which secularists often fall. Christian ethics, in its true and complete form, has surely always 'put the emphasis' in quite another place from that of the 'professional moralists' of whom Mr. Russell speaks. Christian morality is not an end but a means. Mr. Russell simplifies his contrast by making it one simply between *inward* and *outward*. 'Professional morality' is for him a kind of egotism: the alternative is to be interested in things and people outside oneself. For the Christian there is a distinction of higher and lower, as well as of inner and outer: (the latter distinction belongs to a somewhat antiquated psychology which used the terms 'extravert' and 'introvert'). And we may note two further points: one, that there seems to be a suggestion that self-denial is not merely a negative activity to be kept in its place, but that it is a repression to be discouraged; and second, that a traditionally or conventionally 'virtuous person' is one absorbed in the pursuit of his own virtue (undefined).

The reason why I have called Mr. Russell's book a gospel of mediocrity is this: that because he finds that the ordinary man or woman is very rarely and not often seriously bothered about the destiny of man, but is in a state fluctuating between happiness and misery, which depends only on his material circumstances and his relations with his family and the people about him, the destiny of man is in consequence something of interest only to those few persons whose futile curiosity (another kind of curiosity than that which Mr. Heard proposes) leads them to worry about such matters. Mr. Russell sets up for our speculative acceptance a theory of life which he believes is that which the majority of men, so far as their self-interest is intelligent, live by. But when such an attitude is exposed in intellectual terms, it becomes something very different from what it is when it is merely lived out. We might say that it is a view of life which is perfectly tenable until it is made articulate. For once we have asked the question: what is the end of man? we have put ourselves beyond the possibility of being satisfied with the answer: 'there isn't any end, and the only thing to do is to be a nice person and get on with your neighbours.'

It is the difference between answering this question negatively, like Mr. Russell, and finding an unsatisfactory answer, like Mr. Heard or Mr.

Read, that marks a difference between two generations of secularists. On the simple political plane,
of course, this difference is between the Socialists
(rationalists) and the Communists. I should say
rather, some Communists, because Communism
is comprehensive enough to find a place for many
who may be spiritually still Socialists: for those
who see it as simply a more efficient machine than
Socialism or Capitalism, for those who are moved
by immediate humanitarian passions, as well as for
those who seek it as a kind of salvation. It will be
observed that although Communism does not
attempt to answer the question: what is the end
of man? and would I presume affirm such a question to be meaningless, it does offer an answer
to another question: what is the end of the individual man or woman? and to many people this
answer seems good enough. It is this answer
which Communism is able to give to the question:
what is the end of the individual? which goes to
account for the 'conversion' of some notable
individualist intellectuals, such as M. André
Gide. There is a possible contrast to be drawn here
between the conversion of intellectuals in the
modern world to Christianity, and their conversion
to Communism. The conversion to Christianity
is apt to be due, I think, to a latent dissatisfaction with all secular philosophy, becoming,
perhaps, with apparent suddenness, explicit and

coherent.[1] A conversion to Communism, on the other hand, may be simply a flight from one extreme to avoid the other; with, on a deeper plane, a desire to satisfy repressed Christian impulses without embracing Christianity. I do not suggest that all cases of conversion can be accounted for in these ways; but I think that the suggestion I have just made would go far to account for M. André Gide. He found his *immoraliste* individualism leading nowhere, or at last to a dead end: and there seemed nothing to do, if he was to avoid Christianity, but to take the other extreme tack.[2] The satisfactions of individualism failing, M. Gide turns to a doctrine which, while it has nothing to say to the question: what is the end of man? can say a good deal about the self-surrender of the individual to society. The *âme collective* does duty for God. It is noteworthy that M. Gide (in spite of his distinguished connexion with Charles Gide) never took the slightest interest in economics, and still professes an utter ignorance of the subject. (He retains the charming frankness that has al-

[1]In this comparison I am deliberately disregarding the operation of grace in order to keep it to the secular plane.

[2]M. Gide's conversion to Communism has been presented as something involving an heroic sacrifice of his creative gifts. It might, of course, be retorted that possibly the exhaustion of M. Gide's creative gifts had something to do with his conversion to Communism.

ways been one of his most admirable qualities.[1])
I cannot help believing that M. Gide's motive was
largely the *desire for his individual salvation*—
which can remain a desire of something for oneself, even when it is a desire to escape from oneself. I am the more inclined to this belief because
M. Gide's writings have always seemed to me to
belong to a class of literature of which they are
neither the first nor the last example: that in
which the author is moved partly by the desire to
justify himself, and partly by the desire to cure
himself. The greatest authors have never written
for these reasons; but among this class is included
much of the best of the second order of writing.[2]

The Marxist mysticism is not the only secular
mysticism that has been propagated in our time.
I do not intend to discuss racial or imperial

[1]According to the *compte rendu* of a debate which took place
a few years ago between M. Gide and some of his non-Commu-
nist critics, he professed to have been moved largely by humanitarian motives. I would not depreciate these, but they do not seem
quite adequate by themselves.

[2]For a fervent expression of the desire for salvation by escape
from individuality, see an essay by Mr. J. Middleton Murry in
a symposium called *Marxism* (Chapman & Hall: 1935). Mr.
Murry may have modified his views since and, even if not, might
wish to rewrite some of his pages: for on p. 105 he says: 'at the
heart of Marxism lies a grim effort at "depersonalisation", which
unless a man has undergone, I do not believe he will ever be a
Marxist save in name. Of course, this is true only for the member
of "bourgeois society" who becomes a Marxist....' But at the

mysticism, as it does not seem philosophically to merit very much attention. The most remarkable, the most ambitious attempt to erect a secular philosophy of life in our time—though of course not the most influential—is that of the late Irving Babbitt. In a survey like this, Babbitt deserves more attention than any of the other writers whom I have mentioned or shall mention. In the first place, Babbitt's motive was awareness of, alarm at, the ills of the modern secular world; and his work as a whole constitutes the most complete and thorough diagnosis of the malady, as it shows itself in literature, in education, in politics and philosophy, that has been made. His learning was not only prodigious but organized so as at every point to reinforce the structure of his thought. He saw connexions that no other mind would have perceived. He was not a system-builder. What makes him unique is that, while himself a disbeliever, even an opponent of re-vealed religion, he attacked the foundations of

end of the same paragraph he says: 'That grim effort at de-personalisation, of which I have spoken, is just as incumbent upon any proletarian who wants to be a Marxist as upon any bour-geois.' Mr. Murry tells us emphatically that the individual is an illusion, and that 'his sole concrete reality is that of a cell of a social organism, governed by unconscious laws'. The point is that Mr. Murry has started with a notion of the 'individual' which is not Christian, in order to end by denying the existence of the individual. He derives Marxism from Spinoza.

secularism more deeply and more comprehensively than any other writer of our time. His mind, on its periphery, touching questions and philosophies of our time, might be the mind of a Christian; and except from a Christian standard, I do not see how we can object to his conclusions. We have to penetrate to the interior to find cause for dissatisfaction.

I have written elsewhere, and some years ago, about the inadequacy of Babbitt's doctrine of the 'higher will' and the 'inner check', and I do not propose to repeat my criticism of Babbitt on these points. But a posthumous essay which was published last year (*The Dhammapada*: *Translated from the Pali with an Essay on Buddha and the Occident*) gives occasion for a review having a closer bearing upon our subject. The problem is why Babbitt, with such a mind and equipment as, it would seem, could only be supported by Christianity, should have turned to Primitive Buddhism (Hinayana) instead. But first it will help us if we can form some conclusion about what he made of Buddhism.

I think that careful attention to this important and interesting essay will disclose a steady, unconscious desire to evade Christian conclusions at any cost, even at the cost of what may seem to others than the author rather important features of Buddhism. One of the reasons why Buddhism appeals to him is apparently his hostility to

Platonic ideas, and his dislike of the Platonic
influence upon Christian theology. 'Buddha is so
disconcerting to us,' he says, 'because doctrinally
he recalls the most extreme of our Occidental
philosophers of the flux, and at the same time, by
the type of life at which he aims, reminds us
rather of the Platonist and of the Christian.' Yet
he recognizes quite clearly that contrast between
the flux and the eternal is quite as vital to Buddhism as to Christianity, for he says later: 'According to Buddha, anything that is impermanent is
not only unreal but finally illusory.' Throughout
the essay he insists upon this difference between
Buddhism and Christianity: that in Buddhism one
can come to a genuine supernaturalism on 'strictly
experimental' grounds, for reasons that are 'not
metaphysical but practical', by knowledge of
'immediate data of consciousness', 'on psychological grounds', by a 'practical and psychological
method'. It is worth while discovering what can,
and cannot, be affirmed on 'strictly experimental'
grounds, or what it means to be a 'critical and
experimental supernaturalist'. When Babbitt says
'supernaturalist', he does not mean a person who
believes in miracles: on that point he is rather
guarded. What is specifically supernatural, he
says, about Buddha and other religious teachers
such as St. Francis, is 'their achievement of certain
virtues'; of which virtues he puts humility at the

head. It turns out a little later that what we have to do with is not humility, but 'the psychic equivalent' of humility, that is, a will that transcends the cosmic order. And he affirms the existence of a 'quality of will' peculiar to man as one of the immediate data of consciousness. He is certain of this, and equally certain that the soul and the existence of God are not immediate data of consciousness. Yet he does not consider the question whether we can talk about immediate data of consciousness unless, as is far from the case, we generally agree as to what they are: otherwise, one man's data may turn out to be another man's constructions.

According to Babbitt's scheme, the primacy of a certain 'quality of will' distinguishes Buddhism. But at this point he is not apparently contrasting Buddhism with Christianity, but with the views of 'Western philosophers' from Descartes down. And he admits that this Buddhistic 'quality of will . . . has been almost inextricably bound up in the Occident with the doctrine of divine grace and has been obscured in direct proportion to the decline of this doctrine'.

We might complain here that since his Buddhism is by assumption a pure Buddhism, uncorrupted by the practices and doctrines of later times, he ought to contrast it with the equally pure Christianity of whatever period he chose; and that we should not be distracted by corruptions or perversions of Christian doctrine, if we are not allowed to consider those of Buddhism. But while this excellent quality of the will has been obscured in the Occident by the decline of the doctrine of grace, yet it is also the will's association with this doctrine that Babbitt objects to. For grace does not appeal to the practical, experimental, realistic mind; although this same practical mind can accept the idea of the 'higher self' as a self 'that one possesses in common with other men'. At this point Babbitt would seem to be very near to Mr. Murry and the mystical Communists: but it is the 'individualism' of Buddha that most powerfully attracts him. He observes:

'The person who assumes a genuinely critical attitude is finally forced to accept in some form or other the maxim that man is the measure of all things. If one is told in the words of Plato that not man but God is the measure of all things, the obvious reply is that man nowhere perhaps gives his own measure so clearly as in his conception of God. . . .'

To which the obvious reply is that this may be an obvious reply, but is a smart and sophistical retort without being an answer. If man gives his own measure in his conception of God, then there must be a God in relation to whom man's conception is measured.

There are moments, indeed, in which Babbitt appears to be offering Buddhism for the serious consideration of the Christian, not as a preferable alternative, but as a complement.

'The true Buddhist, like the true Christian, takes a gloomy view of the unconverted man.

'His paradox of true self-love, interpreted in the light of renunciation, does not turn out so very differently from the Christian paradox of dying that one may live.

'In general, a collateral benefit of any comprehension one may achieve of Buddha is that it will help one to a better understanding of Christ.

'Religion also looks upon life as a process of adjustment. This process as envisaged by the Christian is summed up once for all in Dante's phrase: "In his will is our peace". A reading of works like the Dhammapada suggests that the psychological equivalent of this form of adjustment was not unknown to Buddha.'

One might remark, about the last of these quotations, that it is not proved that there can be any 'psychological equivalent'; and it leads us further to remark that Babbitt sometimes appears to be unaware of differences as well as of resemblances between Buddhism and Christianity. His observations about Christian mysticism suggest that there is perhaps one gap in his immense reading; certainly in his understanding. But his relative estimate of the two religions may be gauged from the following:

'It would seem desirable, then, that those who object on either humanistic or religious grounds to the overreaching attitude of scientific naturalists should not burden themselves with any unnecessary metaphysical or theological baggage, and that their appeal should be to experience rather than to some counter dogma.'

Which must be taken as a downright rejection of revelation.

Now, one very remarkable fact strikes the reader the moment he has finished this essay. When Babbitt speaks of Christianity he is apt to be thinking of some of the decayed forms of religiosity that he had seen about him, yet he is concerned with a faith that men had been professing to live by during nearly two thousand years. When he speaks of Buddhism, he is dealing with a refined abstraction, with the texts of the master's sayings. He is comparing not Buddha and Christ, or Buddhism and Christianity, but Buddha and Christianity. And there is a still more remarkable oversight. I do not think that his argument, or rather persuasion, is so much invalidated by his rejection of what came after Buddha, as by his ignoring of what came before. Buddha may be regarded as a reformer of a religion that had been in existence for a long time before him, and one of the assumptions of that religion was the doctrine of reincarnation. Babbitt says in passing: 'A Buddha is supposed to be immediately aware not merely of his own karma, but, at will, of the karma of others.' But he does not tell us whether he himself believes in karma and in reincarnation, or in the doctrine that there have been many Buddhas. One would like to know whether these are questions of 'unnecessary metaphysical and theological baggage', or of experience. Whether the Buddha himself believed in these doctrines is not quite the point either: the point is that re-incarnation was so deep in the mentality of his hearers as to be a category of their thought, and that his teaching assumes its truth. And it is as essential to Buddhism as the future states of heaven and hell are to Christianity.

'Knowledge in matters religious waits upon will.' That seems to me to state, though perhaps one-sidedly, a very important truth. The more intelligent and sensitive the secularist is, the more clearly manifest in him is the deflection of will. And that sentence also I have quoted from Babbitt's essay on Buddhism.

I suggest that the Buddhism of Irving Babbitt is not simply a *purified* Buddhism, essence of Buddhism freed from all gross superstitions and made palatable for the intellectual and cultivated modern man: but that it is an artificial Buddhism

—not only purified but *canned*; separated from all the traditional ways of behaving and feeling which went to make it a living religion in its own environments, which made it a religion possible for every level of intelligence and sensibility from the highest to the lowest. It therefore has something in common with the *psychological mysticism* that is a phenomenon of decadence rather than of growth. This is the mysticism which seeks contact with the sources of supernatural power, divorced from religion and theology; the mysticism which must always be suspect, and which sometimes springs up in cults whose aims are not far removed from those of magic.

It is significant that this psychological mysticism has recently appeared in the work of a writer very far removed from Irving Babbitt in attitude, a writer the majority of whose works Babbitt would probably have associated with much of what he disapproved. The mixture of violent prejudice with sympathetic interest in Christianity displayed in the writings of Babbitt has a curious analogue in the writings of Mr. Aldous Huxley. Most of our Communists show indifference, rather than hostility, to Christianity: an indifference only possible on a foundation of ignorance, insensibility and incuriosity. Mr. Huxley is neither ignorant, insensitive nor incurious; he has attempted to maintain an intelligent scepticism in a world of increasing barbarism. He has often written about Christianity, breathing a kind of low fire and chilly fury that seem to indicate that it has some interest for him. It is interesting, therefore, after considering Babbitt on the Dhammapada, to read the last page of Mr. Huxley's Peace Pamphlet (*What Are You Going to Do About It?*). Here we find him advocating the practice of 'meditation' (to which Babbitt also was devoted) specifically for the purpose of bringing about the Will to Peace.

'The sources of the will lie below the level of consciousness in a mental region where intellect and feeling are largely inoperative. Whatever else they may be—and many theological and psychological theories have been elaborated in order to explain their nature and their mode of action—religious rites, prayer and meditation are devices for affecting the sources of the will. It is a matter of empirical experience that regular meditation on, say, courage or peace often helps the meditator to be brave and serene. Prayer for moral strength and tenacity of purpose is in fact quite often answered. Those who, to express in symbolic action their attachment to a cause, take part in impressive ceremonies and rites, frequently come away strengthened in their power to resist temptations and make sacrifices for the cause. There is good evidence that the practice of some

kind of spiritual exercise in common is extremely
helpful to those who undertake it. . . . Meditation
is a psychological technique whose efficacy does
not depend on previous theological belief. It can
be successfully practised by anyone who is prepared to take the necessary trouble.'

This is a very interesting statement. I am certainly not one to deny that 'meditation is a
psychological technique whose efficacy does not
depend on previous theological belief'. I only
maintain that if it neither depends on previous
theological belief nor leads towards it, then it is a
technique that must be very suspect indeed. It
may turn out to be merely an occult means of
getting one's own way; it may foster the *libido
dominandi*. Mr. Huxley would be the last to deny
this; only he would insist that to meditate to bring
about peace is obviously to meditate for a good
cause. So far, so good: but from a Christian point
of view—from any religious point of view—it
cannot be an ultimate good cause, inasmuch as
peace itself (the peace of this world) is not an end
but a means. There is apt to be impurity of
motives in our *natural* devotion even to such a
good cause as peace; and in the effort to purify
our motives towards peace, the effort to isolate
for contemplation the essential idea of peace, we
must, I think, be led to the final theological problem of the end of man. Otherwise, it is an en-

deavour to employ great and unknown forces for immediate and inadequate ends: and that seems to me to be putting ourselves in the utmost spiritual danger. It is an even greater temptation than that of the eudemonism, possibly ataraxy, to which the meditation of Babbitt might lead.

I have not, however, introduced the mysticism of Mr. Huxley for its own interest, and still less in order to discuss the problem of peace, but as a bit of evidence for the thesis that secularism today is not a solid force of disciplined troops, but a varied host of allegiances. And I might say at this point that I do not mean by secularism primarily the various distractions from the Christian life, the various temptations to live on a simply animal level, which occasion so much distress to the faithful. I am not concerned with the cinema, or the press, or the wireless, or the degrading influences of a mechanized civilization. These are serious enough, but they constitute a minor problem. They represent merely the contemporary form—though it may be a form more powerful and oppressive than any before—of the permanent force of the world against which the spirit must always struggle. I am concerned with the ideas, the philosophies however inchoate, which either tolerate these things or fail to oppose them in the right way. For we must remember that almost every secular philosophy or social system, even those which we must regard as definitely hostile, is itself opposed to *some* of the features of contemporary society that we ourselves condemn.

The fact is that the situation of belief in the modern world is more analogous to that of the later Roman Empire than to any other period that we know. And one of the features of resemblance is the psychological mysticism of which I have been speaking.

There are many other philosophies individually worthy of discussion; and of course this paper would be neater if I did not confine myself almost altogether to examples from England and America, but considered men individually equally important in other countries. I know that I ought to have something to say about Stefan George, and certainly Max Scheler and possibly Friedrich Gundolf; and I ought to have given a succinct historical account of how things came to be as they are, without failing to give due space to Schopenhauer, Wagner and Nietzsche. I should touch upon Schleiermacher and Feuerbach, and I should have a long footnote about Logical Positivism, speculating how much it owes to G. E. Moore on the one hand, and Brentano, Husserl, Meinong and Heidegger on the other. But this is a paper, and not a book; and it is a paper written for a special occasion. It seems to me therefore proper to use the material that is ready in my mind, without either taking time to refresh my memory of authors whom I have read only once, or still less mug up works that I have never read at all. So before making my concluding observations, I shall consider one man who cannot be omitted, an Englishman who cannot be duplicated or replaced by a specimen from any other country, whose position is unique, and whose peculiar attitude towards Christianity does not seem to me to have been quite correctly estimated. That is D. H. Lawrence.

The point is that the will to get out from Christianity into a religion of one's own operated in Lawrence as it operated in Babbitt. The extreme differences between the two men (how they would have disliked each other) account easily for their decamping in quite opposite directions; but there is a certain similarity in the motive. Both men sprang from environments which (however different in other ways) gave them an early experience of Christianity at anything but its best; and they failed ever completely to see Christianity as anything but the Christianity that entered into their early and important sensitive experience. Less passionate and powerful men, in a similar way on their own level, have gone through life unable to identify Christianity with anything more than the unpleasant smell of their school chapel, or a particular preceptor whom they disliked. We have found in Babbitt a suspiciously determined will not to be taken in— a will to be 'modern', 'empirical' and 'experimental' at all costs, even the cost of using such words only as emotional exclamations. Lawrence is less complicated and in some respects less interesting. His will against Christianity is easier to understand. For Babbitt was by nature an educated man, as well as a highly well-informed one: Lawrence, even had he acquired a great deal more knowledge and information than he ever came to possess, would always have remained uneducated. By being 'educated' I mean having such an apprehension of the contours of the map of what has been written in the past, as to see instinctively where everything belongs, and approximately where anything new is likely to belong; it means, furthermore, being able to allow for all the books one has not read and the things one does not understand—it means some understanding of one's own ignorance. With these two odd handicaps—the will against Christianity that was a residue of childhood and adolescence, and the temperament of *un*education —Lawrence started out on a lifelong search for a religion.

Whatever his disadvantages, a man of the ability of Lawrence, and with such an addiction, can be of very great value indeed; and it is as an investigator of the religious life—as a kind of *contemplative* rather than a theologian—that he seems to me to take a high place with most right. People have deplored the spoiling of the remarkable novelist of *Sons and Lovers* for the making of a medicine man; but much as I admire that rather sickly and morally unintelligible book, I find the medicine man much more important than the novelist. Mr. Aldous Huxley, in his admirable preface to Lawrence's collected letters,[1] says 'Lawrence was always and unescapably an artist'. He does not seem to me an artist at all, but a man with a sketch-book: his poetry, very interesting amateur work, is only notes for poems. Mr. Huxley says significantly a little later: 'the fact of his being an artist explains a life which seems, when you forget it, inextricably strange.' The truth is, of course, that an artist needs to live a commonplace life if he is to get his work done —a life far more of routine, and indeed less 'inextricably strange' than that of a politician or a stockbroker. An artist may have elements in his composition that drive him towards excesses of one kind or another, but a failure to keep these in hand leads to a failure in his art. But I think of Lawrence neither as an artist, nor as a man who failed to be an artist; I think of him, as I have

[1]Reprinted in Mr. Huxley's recent volume of essays, *The Olive Tree*.

suggested, as a researcher into religious emotion. And unless we see him as this, we are apt to attach too much importance to his views on sex and on society, to his psychological extravaganzas, and to personal peculiarities which may account for his aberrations. With the criticism of Lawrence's particular doctrines—his feminism,[1] his *âme collective*, his unconscious, I am for the most part in agreement with Mr. Wyndham Lewis in the section of his *Paleface* that he devotes to Lawrence. But I think that something valuable remains, if we know how to use it.

In the oscillation—of which I shall speak presently—of secular philosophies between antithetical extremes, there is one pair of opposites which it is pertinent to mention at this point. The human mind is perpetually driven between two desires, between two dreams each of which may be either a vision or a nightmare: the vision and nightmare of the material world, and the vision and nightmare of the immaterial. Each may be in turn, or for different minds, a refuge to which to fly, or a horror from which to escape. We desire and fear both sleep and waking; the day brings relief from the night, and the night brings relief from the day; we go to sleep as to death,

[1]The most objectionable feature of *Lady Chatterley's Lover* is surely the view of the male as merely an instrument for the purposes of the female.

and we wake as to damnation. We move, outside of the Christian faith, between the terror of the purely irrational and the horror of the purely rational. Lawrence had a really extraordinary capacity for being exacerbated by the modern world of enlightenment and progress, whether in a Midland mining village or in metropolitan intellectual society. This world was his nightmare; he wanted a world in which religion would be real, not a world of church congresses and religious newspapers, not even a world in which a religion could be *believed*[1], but a world in which religion would be something deeper than belief, in which life would be a kind of religious behaviourism. Hence the prancing Indians, who, in *Mornings in Mexico*, inspired some of his finest and most brilliant writing. He wished to go as low as possible in the scale of human consciousness, in order to find something that he could assure himself was *real*.

The attempt is fundamentally chimerical. We

[1]Compare, for a very different attitude to a similar apprehension, the words of Dom John Chapman (*Spiritual Letters*, p. 47): '. . . the *corresponding trial* of our contemporaries seems to be the *feeling of not having any faith*; not temptations against any particular article (usually), but a mere feeling that religion is not true. It is an admirable purgative, just as the eighteenth century one was; it takes all pleasure out of spiritual exercises, and strips the soul naked. It is very unpleasant.' Lawrence saw no need for standing up to this. It would be unfair to say that he ran away; because it never occurred to him that there was any other course to take.

do not feel that Lawrence really got inside the skin of his Hopis, nor would we wish him to do so, because he was a civilized and sensitively conscious man, and his Indians, one feels, are pretty stupid. He merely gave a marvellous record of how the Indians affected Lawrence. Yet his mistaken attempt was the result of an awareness of something very important. He was aware that religion is not, and can never survive as, simply a code of morals. It has not even much meaning to say that religion is 'good'. Other things are good or bad in relation to one's religion. If (I think he would have said) you find you can only accept an 'evil' religion, then for God's sake do, for that is far nearer the truth than not having any. For what the evil religion has in common with the good is more important than the differences; and it is more important really to feel terror than to sing comminatory psalms. So he set himself, by an immense effort of will—the same effort that the Christian has to make towards a different end—to believe in nature spirits, and to try to worship stocks and stones. And with the same perseverance he set himself to an attitude of scepticism towards science, for he saw that science only provides a relative truth, and as we cannot know the relations, we do better—the contemporary mind being what it is—to deny it altogether than to accept it as an absolute which it is not.

The religion of Lawrence can be a useful criterion for us in testing the reality of our own faith: it can serve as a constant reminder that Christianity is frightening, frightful and scandalous to that secular mind which we are all compelled to some extent to share. But for itself, it remains on the level of secularism, because it remains a religion of power and magic. Or rather, the religion which Lawrence would have liked to achieve is a religion of power and magic, of control rather than propitiation. What he, being a civilized man, actually arrived at, was, of course, only a religion of autotherapy. It was like the restless search of the hypochondriac for a climate in which he can be cured, or in which at least he can bear his ailments more easily. Perhaps there is this motive in all of us, but if so, at least we can hope that our being aware of it helps to keep it in its place. We can cry, *Thou son of David, have mercy on me*, but we can be healed only if our faith is stronger even than our desire to be healed.

The purpose of this brief, and no doubt apparently capricious, review has been primarily to make the point that we are not suffering today simply from 'loss of faith'—a loss of faith which brings with it inexorably a lowered vitality—but from a strong and positive misdirection of the will. I have been concerned chiefly with individualistic

34

misdirections of will, not with the collective mis-directions of a political nature; but the latter must be kept in mind also. I should now like to detail what seem to me the principal characteristics of philosophies without revelation.[1]

The first characteristic is *instability*. Were there a science of social psychology, it would no doubt provide a set of convenient terms in which to explain the necessity of impermanence. But we may say that any philosophy of life which is the construct of any individual mind, must be con-ditioned by a great deal of which that individual is unconscious. A man is never pure mind, his mind is conditioned by his sensibility and his physical constitution. It is observable that while impersonality of thought is at best only an ideal towards which some approximation can be reached, in modern philosophy divorced from theology this ideal itself has been surrendered. We are able even to have the *aesthetic* attitude to-wards philosophy, so that the work of an individual philosopher can be enjoyed, not for whatever in it may be true, but as an artistic presentation of the personality of the philosopher. There are, of

[1]One might mention at this point the characteristics of those religions which are non-historical. But it does not fall within the scope of this paper, which is concerned with secularism, to expound the view (implicit in what I say) that revelation in the complete sense is the Incarnation. I refer the reader to the essay in this book by the Archbishop of York.

course, group-personalities apparent in philosophy as well as individual personalities—so that it is said that Oxford and Cambridge philosophers are unable to understand each other. This is in part a healthy reaction against the 'lonely thinker' (Spinoza polishing lenses, the Sage of Koenigsberg, Marx in the British Museum), for of all thinkers the lonely one is likely to be the most controlled by the part of himself he knows nothing about. But however much we get together, we can by human means alone arrive only at the kind of fixity and unanimity of belief which might be attributed to a hive of bees. Ultimately, apart from revelation, there would seem to be no criterion of philosophic credibility.

The second characteristic is *recurrence*. The same philosophies tend to reappear again and again, sometimes by deliberate revival, but perhaps more often unconsciously. We easily believe that something is quite new when it is merely a new form, adapted to place and time, of some doctrine of antiquity. Those who yearn for an earthly paradise have to maintain that the key to human problems has been found for the first time.

The third characteristic is involved in the second: it is *the tendency* of each extreme philosophy *to evoke an opposite*, and sometimes to turn into it by an imperceptible metamorphosis. Thus you get an oscillation between individualism and collectivism; between rationalism and intuitivism; and an immoderate humanitarianism may lead to cruelty and tyranny. All these things spring from titanism, or the attempt to build a purely human world without reliance upon grace.

The fourth characteristic of secular philosophies is *immediate results*. It is easy to invent philosophies that will appear to the uneducated to be more promising than Christianity: which will appear more feasible, valid either for the inventors individually, or for a limited group or under transient conditions of time and place. Secular philosophies must inevitably, in the atmosphere of the modern world, have a seductiveness with which Christianity cannot compete. They are always presented as new, and as capable of setting things right at once.

We must remember also that the choice between Christianity and secularism is not simply presented to the innocent mind, *anima semplicetta*, as to an impartial judge capable of choosing the best when the causes have both been fully pleaded. The whole tendency of education (in the widest sense—the influences playing on the common mind in the forms of 'enlightenment') has been for a very long time to form minds more and more adapted to secularism, less and less equipped to apprehend the doctrine of revelation and its consequences. Even in works of Christian apologetic, the assumption is sometimes that of the secular mind.[1] Any apologetic which presents the Christian faith as a *preferable alternative* to secular philosophy, which fights secularism on its own ground, is making a concession which is a preparation for defeat. Apologetic which proceeds from part to part of the body of Christian belief, testing each by itself according to secular standards of credibility, and which attempts to constitute Christian belief as a body of acceptable parts, so as to end by placing the least possible burden upon faith, seems to me to be a reversal of the proper method. Should we not first try to apprehend the meaning of Christianity as a whole, leading the mind to contemplate first the great gulf between the Christian mind and the secular habits of thought and feeling into which, so far as we fail to watch and pray, we all tend to fall? When we have appreciated the awfulness of this difference, we are in a better position to examine

[1]For instance, the doctrine of the damnation of unbaptized infants has been commonly rejected in recent times simply because it is repugnant. But the development of the state of mind to which this doctrine is repugnant must itself be examined before we can accept it with confidence; and the question of the repugnance of a doctrine is not the same as that of its truth. This is perhaps the extreme case, but it is obviously very dangerous to rely on a sentiment of recent growth, especially when the higher religious emotions have certainly tended to atrophy or occlusion.

the body of our belief analytically, and consider what is permanent truth, and what is transient or mistaken. As even the disciples, during the life of our Lord and immediately after His death and resurrection, suffered from occasional lapses of faith, what are we to expect of a world in which the will has been powerfully and increasingly misdirected for a long time past? What a discursive reading of the literature of secularism, over a number of years, leads me to believe, however, is that the religious sentiment—which can only be completely satisfied by the complete message of revelation—is simply suffering from a condition of repression painful for those in whom it is repressed, who yearn for the fulfilment of belief, although too ashamed of that yearning to allow it to come to consciousness.

II

By the Rev. Prof. KARL BARTH

*Translated by the Rev. J. O. Cobham, Principal, and
the Rev. R. J. C. Gutteridge, Tutor, of the
Queen's College, Edgbaston, Birmingham*

Anyone who proposes to expound the Christian
apprehension of revelation inevitably places himself, and all those who are willing to listen to him,
within a quite definite sphere, in which a well
defined discipline or order holds good. Should this
prove uncongenial to him he is, of course, perfectly free to proceed no further. But if he should
wish to proceed further, he is not at liberty to do
so on his own terms, heedless of the sphere within
which he must work and the discipline under
which he must remain. Even a Jew or a pagan or
an unbeliever can only properly come to grips
with the Christian apprehension of revelation by
working hypothetically within that sphere, and by
remaining hypothetically under that discipline.
No doubt it is arguable whether an apprehension
that is only hypothetical is as a matter of fact possible. For if the apprehension is merely hypothetical it must, be it as relevant as it may, prove

but an unfruitful and indeed ultimately a dead apprehension. The fact remains, however, that a living and fruitful Christian apprehension of revelation can only be attained on the condition that we do our thinking and expounding relevantly, and that means within that sphere and under that discipline.

They tell me of so-called 'laymen' who find theological language—perhaps even the language of this essay?—terribly difficult. It may well be that theological language is sometimes unnecessarily difficult. But it may also be that the so-called 'laymen' (and their theological councillors!) are in the habit of deploring theological language only because they rebel against the sphere and the discipline within which Christians, if they are really theologians and Christians, *must* think and speak. I would advise 'laymen' and theologians who will not admit that only within that quite definite sphere and under that quite definite discipline is it possible to speak of the Christian understanding of revelation, to put this essay aside without further delay.

The Christian apprehension of revelation is the response of man to the Word of God whose name is Jesus Christ. It is the Word of God who creates the Christian apprehension of revelation. From Him it gains its content, its form and its limit. That is indeed what the adjective 'Christian' implies, and thereby the field under consideration is imperiously defined and all discussion about it is ruled out. For the Christian apprehension of revelation is that apprehension which is bound up with the name of Jesus Christ. An apprehension of revelation which had been detached from this bond would not as such be the Christian one, though it might perhaps be the Jewish or the Stoic or perhaps the Romantic or the Positivist— at all events, it would be some other apprehension of revelation. But it is just under this bondage to the name of Jesus Christ that the Christian apprehension of revelation finds its *freedom*. It is under no other law than that which is dictated to it through this name. It is not necessary first to look for the true revelation on the right hand or on the left: much less is it necessary first to ask whether there is such a thing as revelation at all. Revelation need not first be brought in from any quarter, or furnished with proof. In the Christian apprehension, revelation is from the very first already known and already possessed. The name Jesus Christ, upon which the Christian apprehension is dependent, affirms that the Christian apprehension has already been found by the revelation. Nor is the Christian apprehension subject to any general truths about God or man, nor about the relation between God and man, since all knowledge of God and of man it has sought and found and ever

43

again seeks and finds in this name. It is not ultimately and finally conditioned by any demand
arising out of the necessities of human living and
the laws of human thinking; it is conditioned, and
that ultimately and fundamentally, only through
the truth that unveils itself in this name. The
Christian apprehension of revelation is a transcript
of the commandment given by God to men. As a
human undertaking this transcript is done upon
the plane of human living and human thinking.
But there the name Jesus Christ, and it alone, can
have the power to rule, to direct and fashion; and
this power no man-made hypothesis can have,
however ideal or ultimate in intention it may be.
Anyone who proposes to expound the Christian
apprehension of revelation, and anyone who is
willing to listen to him on this subject, would
therefore be well advised to bring himself under
control, just as a rider brings his mount under
control—that is to say, to bring himself to an
attitude of attention, of awe, of trust, of obedience
to this name. Every weakening of this initial
attitude would go to endanger this apprehension
and even to render it impossible.

I. THE ESSENCE OF REVELATION

The name Jesus Christ defines the revelation as
one that has taken place and that still takes place

in the event of the existence of Him who bears this name. To know anything about revelation in the original, true and strict sense of the concept, we must know about Jesus Christ. 'Revelations' which are different from that which has taken place and that which is still taking place in Him, we can only call 'revelations' in a perverted, invalid and loose sense of the concept. The discussion as to whether there is not revelation also in 'other religions' is superfluous. We need not hesitate to grant this to them, for revelation to them clearly means something very different. But then the *Christian* understanding of revelation must be very exactly differentiated from what is understood by revelation in these 'other religions'. The difference is this—that in Jesus Christ, and in Him alone, there enters upon the stage of human life that which is really *new*, and that which is hitherto unknown, because veiled and hidden. Revelation is here something other than an exaggerated expression for the unexpected and astounding appearance and discovery of a *best example* in an otherwise familiar sequence of development. It is no recollection (*anamnesis*) of the Idea, in the Platonic sense, of such a sequence—an idea that has perhaps been forgotten, but is not fundamentally unknown. Revelation (*apokalypsis, phanerosis, revelatio*) really means here what the word itself implies, viz., the appearance of that which is

45

new; the appearance, therefore, of that which is in no wise known before. That which is new is primarily Jesus Christ Himself, His person in its concrete *reality*. This His concrete reality, simply as a concrete reality, towers above every other reality in virtue of its being unique in kind and of its having taken place once for all. It is, as the New Testament says, ἐφ' ἅπαξ. There are indeed tokens of this reality, there are witnesses and testimonies to it, but it has no analogies and is nowhere repeated. It stands alone and it speaks for itself. It receives light from nowhere else; the source of its light is in itself and in itself alone. This newness of Jesus Christ must not, however, be understood to mean that His person was ultimately merely the appearance of a nature with which we are familiar apart from Him, even if it is regarded as the highest appearance and best example of it. Nor must it be understood to mean that He was the supreme realization of a general potentiality, even if He be regarded as for this reason unique. One must ask the representatives of the 'other religions' whether by revelation they do not *at the best* mean this—the highest manifestation of an idea, of a general potentiality. Just as the reality is new, so too is the *potentiality* which is presupposed and realized in the reality of the person of Jesus Christ. It is a potentiality that is God's and not ours, that is known to God and not to us.

Hence Jesus Christ is indeed the fulfilment of divine prophecy; He is not, however, the fulfilment of human yearnings, of human demands and of human speculations. He is, indeed, the manifestation of the eternal wisdom of God; but He is not the verification of the *a priori* wit of man. There is certainly a divinely posited potentiality of His existence and of the knowledge of His existence; but there is no standard by which we can measure Him, no point from which we can survey Him, no principle by means of which we can judge Him. If we are free to set our human presuppositions, as though they were absolute, over against Him; or, to put this otherwise, if we are not free, if we are unable to set our human presuppositions, because they are relative, over against Him; or again, if we really imagine that we can and should measure Him, survey Him, pass judgment upon Him and therefore master Him—all these can only be symptoms of the fact that the reality and the potentiality of His person are both still hidden from us. For if the divine potentiality of His existence were known to us, how could we desire to exalt ourselves above Him in this fashion? And if the divine potentiality of His existence is unknown to us, this very fact betrays that even the reality of His existence is unknown to us, and that Jesus Christ is still in truth hidden from us. We are then speaking about Jesus Christ only in

47

appearance; we are speaking in reality and under misuse of His name about one of the deities on whose revelation the 'other religions' base themselves; and it should not then surprise us, if in our encounter with these we should find ourselves embarrassed. But if He is not hidden from us, His potentiality will be as new to us as His reality, and we shall make no attempt to master Him. It is precisely this complete newness of His appearing that marks the revelation as revelation in the original, true and strict meaning of the concept. What point is there then in applying the word revelation to something whose potentiality and presupposition we already know *before* we know the revelation—as the astronomers already knew the orbit of Sirius before we had discovered the star itself? If it is not wholly new to us, even as a possibility, how then can it be a revelation to us? But just on that account we must say that only the man who knows about Jesus Christ knows anything at all about revelation. Any attitude towards Jesus Christ that could envisage accepting or rejecting Him as possible alternatives would therefore immediately be another symptom of the fact that we know nothing whatsoever about revelation. For revelation to which analogies can be drawn, revelation which can be repeated, revelation which merely conforms to a general potentiality, is not revelation. Hence, there being no possibility of mastering Him, revelation will be discerned in Jesus Christ or it will just not be discerned at all.

The assertion of the newness of the person of Jesus Christ and therefore the assertion that He, and He alone, is to be called revelation in the original, true and strict meaning of the concept, cannot however itself result from general considerations and reflections. For a doctrine which rested on the basis of general considerations and reflections would certainly operate only as a strong assertion which would necessarily be opposed by a corresponding and equally strong doubt. But the assertion of the revelation in Jesus Christ, if intended in the original, true and strict sense of the term 'revelation', does not in its origin rest upon the basis of general considerations and reflections, and for that very reason it is not to be attacked, let alone demolished, on this ground. On the contrary, the doctrine has its origin in the recognition of the person of Jesus Christ as the eternal Word of God who was made flesh. This recognition means in general at least this, that revelation is *grace for sinners*. And grace for sinners means an especial, free, unmerited and unearned act of divine turning towards, and condescension to, man. The Word is eternal: it is itself God. Precisely in the recognition of Jesus Christ and therefore in the recognition that the Word was made flesh, we shall say, not that the Word *had* to be made flesh, but that this is actual and potential in virtue of God's free *compassion*; and we shall also say that, *but for* this free compassion the eternal Word would be eternally *hidden* from us. The grace of God made manifest in Jesus Christ necessarily brings us into *Judgment*; it lays us bare as those who are not worthy and who are consequently incapable of perceiving the Word of God in His naked Godhead—as eternally He is in God and is God—to be indeed the Word of God. The man who has received grace, and therefore recognizes that he has need of grace and that he is utterly an object of divine mercy, cannot at any rate conceive of himself as one who discovers and receives a direct revelation. No: and he cannot conceive of himself, either, as one who receives and discovers even an *indirect* revelation other than the revelation which is in Jesus Christ. He will indeed acknowledge that the same eternal Word of God, who was made flesh, is to be perceived in creation as the first work of God, and is therefore to be perceived in nature, in history and in his own heart, conscience and understanding. But he will go further and acknowledge to his own shame that in actual fact he never has perceived the Word in these things, and that moreover he neither can nor ever will perceive it in them. He will certainly not make this admission on the basis of some critical theory of knowledge, but, once again, in the recognition of Jesus Christ as the Word made flesh; in the recognition of the fact that it was God's good pleasure to reveal His Word in this wholly different way; in recognition that he has received grace, and therefore stands in need of grace. In making this recognition he will certainly not consider himself capable of perceiving the Word of God in God's creation. As one who has been brought by grace under judgment, he will on the contrary confess that in that sphere he has always heard and always will hear nothing but the voices of the gods, that is to say, the God-created elements of this world; the voice of earth and of animal life; the voice of the apparently infinite heavens and, sounding through this voice, the voice of the heavens' apparently inescapable fate; the voice of his own blood and of the blood of his parents and of his ancestors flowing in his veins; the voice of the genius and of the hero in his own breast: voices all falsely endowed with divine dignity and authority, and for that very reason, not the eternal Word of God!

The conception of an indirect revelation in nature, in history and in our self-consciousness is destroyed by the recognition of grace, by the recognition of Jesus Christ as the eternal Word who was made flesh: but nothing else destroys it. Accordingly, just in so far as we are blind to this recognition, do we necessarily begin to place fresh confidence in ourselves, and therefore to range by the side of Jesus Christ, first all kinds of indirect revelation and then all kinds of direct revelation too. When this happens the doctrine of the newness of the person of Jesus Christ, and consequently the doctrine that He and He alone may with full seriousness be called revelation, will cease to be clear to us and will barely be defensible. But once we are prepared to recognize the one and only way which was adopted by God to reveal Himself in Jesus Christ, the way of the Word made flesh, the doctrine becomes easy and obvious. For if we come to have confidence in God through this way, the way in which it is given to us to know ourselves as sinners who have received grace, the self-confidence that makes us want to glory in all kinds of other indirect or direct revelations is *ipso facto* taken from us. We can set ourselves against the recognition of grace in Jesus Christ, for that is a bitter recognition indeed. We can wish we were something other and better than mere objects of divine compassion and that alone. In that case it is open to us to glory in revelations. Some natural theology or other may easily be found to take up the tale with greater or less noise and effect. But once we have arrived at the recognition of Jesus Christ, and therefore at the recognition that we have received grace and stand in need of grace, such a course is impossible. Rather the confession becomes inevitable that Jesus Christ *alone* is the revelation.

Jesus Christ is the revelation because He is the *grace* of God made manifest to us—grace in the full sense of the conception. Revelation means that God, without ceasing to be God, was made *man*, 'flesh'. 'Flesh' means man like us in all the finitude, infirmity and helplessness that characterizes our human life and results from our utter distance from God. Revelation means grace. Grace means condescension. Condescension means being made man. Being made man means being made flesh. Jesus Christ is all that. And that, and that alone, is revelation. If God were not *gracious* (and this means if He retained the majesty of His Godhead for Himself), if He did not of His own free decision turn towards men, there would be no revelation; man would be left to himself. If God's grace were not complete, if that grace did not consist in an inconceivably real *descent* of God into our depths, there would be no revelation. If God had not descended so far into these depths that He met us as one of ourselves in all the distance and nearness of a *human form*, there would be no revelation. If He had not become in all respects a *man like ourselves*, and consequently 'flesh', there would be no revelation. All this in very truth God has done for us in Jesus Christ. We acknowledge the *grace* of

God, in that we confess that the eternal Word of the Father, the Lord of heaven and earth, was born and suffered, was crucified, dead and buried. We acknowledge God's true and sole revelation just in the fact that we acknowledge the true *manhood* of Jesus Christ.

But we must not stop here. Jesus Christ is revelation, for the reason that He is the grace of *God*, made manifest to us in the full sense of the conception 'God'. In that He becomes and is man, He is the Lord, who has made us and without whom we are not. He is the Lord of the world, the Lord of all lords of this world. Revelation means the grace of God. But God's grace means the presence and the act of God Himself. God Himself, however, means the Lord. But the Lord means: the One, the Unchangeable, the Eternal, the Almighty, the Maker of heaven and earth. That and that alone is revelation. If man felt himself for a single moment obliged to doubt that the grace which he has received was the *grace of God*, not only would there be no revelation but he would feel himself abandoned. If He who encounters man in revelation and acts upon him were not the *Creator*, but only one who belongs like man himself to God's created world; there would be no revelation. If it were but a demigod or an angel or a man exalted in some special way, whom man encountered in revelation, there would be no revelation. If God Himself in the fullness of His *glory* did not will to meet us and make Himself known to us in revelation, there would be no revelation. But it is just this that He has done for us in Jesus Christ. We acknowledge the grace of *God*, in that we confess that this Man was conceived of the Holy Ghost, born of the Virgin Mary, and that on the third day He rose again from the dead, He ascended into heaven, and sitteth on the right hand of God the Father. In that we acknowledge the true *Godhead* of Jesus Christ, we acknowledge the true and sole revelation of God.

The decisive point can and must now be made. Jesus Christ is the revelation because He is, as the grace of God made manifest, the way, the only way, by which men may come to know God and by which a relationship, and more than this, a communion, between man and God is established. Jesus Christ is the revelation, because in His existence He is *the reconciliation*. Only as he beholds the reconciliation that has taken place between God and man, can *man* know *God*. Anything that man may imagine he knows about God apart from reconciliation, that is to say in his 'natural' position as a rebel against God and consequently under the wrath of God, is in truth but the idol of his own heart. Between God and that man stands, shrouding all things in gloom, his sin. The existence of Jesus Christ is the reconciliation, and therefore the bridging of the gulf that has opened here. And the way in which this comes about is that in Jesus Christ God Himself steps into the place of sinful man, while sinful man is for his part translated into the place of God.

God steps into the place of sinful man. Jesus Christ is true man, man like us. But, as man like us, He acts in a way which is altogether different from the way in which we act. In His humiliation, in His sufferings and death, He espouses the lost condition of mankind and acknowledges the righteousness of the wrath and the judgment of God. He submits to the baptism of repentance. He justifies God against Himself. He calls to God out of the depths and praises His grace alone. Guiltless—and it is precisely in this, His bowing to the judgment of God in which He differentiates Himself from us, that He proves His sinlessness! —He bears our uncleanness and the punishment it involves, and makes it His very own. And since it is He, the eternal Word of God, who does this, the uncleanness and the punishment is now, and this most truly, no longer ours but His. There has taken place once and for all what had to take place if there was to be expiation, if our sins were to be covered, to be washed away, to be forgiven. If the sin is His, if God has taken possession of it, then it is no more ours. So when we remember our sins we are summoned to think no more about ourselves, but about Him who once for all has borne our sin upon the cross and carried it to the grave.

And sinful man is translated to the place of God. That is the other side of the same fact. Jesus Christ is very God. But, just because He is very God, He does not retain the majesty of His Godhead for Himself; rather in the majesty of His Godhead He espouses man in his baseness, man in his suffering and dying, man in his position as one under judgment, man in his subjection to death, man in his utter need of grace. It is indeed this man, this 'flesh', that the eternal Word of God in the person of Jesus Christ has accepted and raised up to unity with Himself. But it is precisely this unity that is signified by the exaltation of this man, accomplished once for all in the resurrection and ascension of Jesus Christ. In Jesus Christ, who is true God, man is snatched from the ordinances and necessities of his mere human nature, and therefore finally and ultimately from death, in order that he may participate in the free, pre-eminent, eternal life of God Himself. In Jesus Christ the glory of God, without ceasing to be God's, has become *our own* as well. But if it is ours, if God has bestowed it on us in Jesus Christ, then we are summoned to seek our life in faith and there to let it be lived, where our life has been made new in Christ and has become our true life. We are summoned to seek our life in faith there, where in the exalted manhood of Jesus Christ we already stand at the right hand of God. This exchange (καταλλαγή) is the reconciliation. It is at once our justification and our sanctification, the remission of our sins and our new birth to a new life. This exchange is the bridging of the gulf between God and man, the dissolution of the darkness, which prevents us from recognizing God, the truth (*aletheia*), and consequently the revelation. Therefore, since this exchange is accomplished in Jesus Christ, He is the true and only revelation of God.

Now it must be admitted that it is by no means obvious that we do recognize in the existence of Jesus Christ the real newness, new even in its potentiality, for what it really is. It is by no means obvious that the grace of God made manifest in Jesus Christ does become judgment for us, and so renders impossible the self-confidence with which we search round for all kinds of other indirect or direct revelations. It is by no means obvious that in Jesus Christ we do recognize very man, and not, say, an idea of man; and very God, and not, say, a demigod; and that we do recognize very God and very man precisely in Jesus Christ. And above all it is by no means obvious that we do recognize in that which has taken place in the death and the resurrection of Christ, that exchange, and therefore our own reconciliation, justification, sanctification and regeneration, as something which has taken place once for all. It is by no means obvious that there is a Christian apprehension of revelation, an apprehension which is the response of man to the Word of God whose name is Jesus Christ. It is by no means obvious that we *believe*. How should we arrive at this response? How should we arrive at faith? Faith is much more than the knowledge that enables us to make this response. Faith is the reference of all our living, thinking, willing and feeling to the existence of Jesus Christ as the one ground upon which we stand, the one stay upon which we hang, the one food by which we are nourished. In the midst of the flux and conflict of human hope and despair, human success and failure, human goodness and evil, human comradeship and loneliness, faith is the ultimate repose, certainty, serenity and hope, which is true and enduring because it is not grounded upon any state, knowledge or action of our own, but upon the existence of Jesus Christ. Faith is our participation in the humanity, in the flesh and blood of Jesus Christ, and thus in the eternal Word of God who has in Christ Jesus made flesh and blood His own, and exalted them to the right hand of God. Faith means life on the basis of that exchange and therefore on the basis of the justification and sanctification which man has received in Jesus Christ. Faith means the life of the man who has been born again in Jesus Christ. The recognition of the revelation, of which we have been speaking, is the recognition given by this faith.

And for this reason it is by no means obvious. Faith admittedly, and with it too the recognition of faith, is a free act of human choice and decision; a work of the heart, the will and the understanding. But, when we are engaged in this work we have no more power to apprehend what we are from our knowledge of ourselves, than we have power to apprehend Jesus Christ from the knowledge which, apart from Him, we have of man and of mankind. Why is it that I believe? Certainly I believe of my own free choice and decision—why should not that be conceded to the pragmatists, psychologists, etc? I am no machine when I believe, but just as certainly I can in so doing apprehend myself only as one who, before he makes his choice, *is chosen*, and as one upon whom, before he himself has decided, a decision *has descended*. What I do as a work of my own heart, will and understanding, can, when I believe, only be done as a *service* to the *Word of God*. It is only in view of all this, in view of the fact that Jesus Christ, very God and very man, interposes with God for me, that I am in a position to stand before God, and walk before Him and respond to His Word. Not for one moment or in any respect can I find occasion for boasting in the fact that I believe and confess that I am called, or that I am ready and able to respond to that call: for that I can only be thankful. The revelation then has proved a revelation to me also, and that by virtue of its own power and decision. The reconciling grace of Jesus Christ has then come to me also as grace which chooses, calls, illuminates and converts, as the grace of the Holy Ghost. How of myself could I tell how I come to believe and make confession? How could I tell how I come to be pardoned? If of myself I had anything to say on the matter it would certainly not be the grace of the Holy Ghost which had come to me; my faith would not then be faith but some sort of religious presumption; my confession not confession but some sort of arbitrary assertion. Of the grace of the Holy Ghost I shall always have only this to say, that I am thankful for it, and that it has come to me as a miracle. And so the Christian apprehension of the essence of revelation will inevitably be consummated in the recognition that, when it does take place, even this apprehension itself takes place only through revelation; or rather that the apprehension is itself revelation, is itself the pouring out of the Holy Ghost, through which the historic incarnation of the Word of God finds its confirmation, through which the ascended Christ shows forth His power and His goodness.

II. THE TOKENS OF REVELATION

Revelation, as the Christian apprehends it, is something that occurs once and for all—once for all just as God is one! It is an occurrence whose subject is and remains God Himself, hence an occurrence whose radiance and power proceeds from itself. Revelation, however, does not occur in heaven but on earth, not in God's eternal sphere, but as the action of God in the human sphere; it takes place amidst the continuity of the occurrences of created things, and that means amidst the occurrences of natural historical life. How otherwise would it be revelation? How otherwise would it consist in the fact that God became man? And it is amidst the same continuity that the revelation actually seeks and finds faith. How otherwise would our faith be a human choice and a freely made decision?

Jesus Christ encounters men humanly and *ipso facto* divinely. And while it is most certainly on the ground of His divinity that men are awakened to faith in Him, it is nevertheless through the medium of His manhood that this awakening takes place. As we have already said, the name, Jesus Christ, the name which is peculiar amongst all other human names, *betokens* the revelation. The man, who, because He is the eternal Word of

62

God, is Himself the revelation, is, considered in Himself, its primary and absolute *means*; He is the Temple, the Robe, the Sword of the eternal Word; He is the *token* that can demonstrate to the human eye, ear and heart 'Here is Emmanuel'. One who believes in Him, believes in the eternal Word of God. But no one would believe in the eternal Word of God, unless this token were given him, unless this name and this man, the flesh and the blood of Jesus Christ, were given. This token by itself would not be revelation. And yet, without this token, the revelation would not be visible and audible to men. Without this token there would be no communication to men, and consequently no revelation.

Now, this primary and absolute token of revelation is in some measure reflected and paralleled, and in this sense repeated, in the sphere of created things, in the sphere of natural lives and historical events. The revelation is but one. But this one revelation has not taken place in vain; it has taken place once and for all. It concerns the whole world, it concerns all men. In that God became man the world has been given a new look. The revelation has imprinted itself upon the nature and the history of this world in quite definite forms, and this it does ever anew. These forms are not revelation itself. They are no multiplications of the Incarnation! They belong entirely to created things, as do all other forms. As tokens of revelation they can be misunderstood and overlooked. Nevertheless, it is just in this their insignificance that, through the revelation, they are what they are; Jesus Christ Himself has instituted and established and determined them, in order that, according to God's good pleasure, they may serve and be effective as tokens of revelation; in order that they may be witnesses and testimonies to Jesus Christ for the purpose of calling men to faith in Him. If this is what the tokens both are and do, then they are this, not by virtue of any power within them or proceeding from them, but by virtue of the power of Jesus Christ, the instruments in Whose hands they are. The power of Jesus Christ is not operative, however, save through these instruments, these secondary and therefore conditioned means of revelation. Just as the power of Christ in their prototype, the humanity of Jesus Christ, is an indirect revelation, so too it is indirect revelation where it is reflected and paralleled in the sphere of other created things.

Here we shall have to think above all of the *words* and *deeds* of Jesus of Nazareth, as they form the subject of the New Testament Gospels. These words and deeds are not themselves the Kingdom of God that 'is at hand'. But both in themselves and in their relation to each other, these words and deeds are the *tokens* of that Kingdom. They bear witness that this Jesus, Who spoke thus and did these miracles, is the Messiah. And here the words of Jesus differentiate His deeds from those of a mere human miracle-monger or thaumaturgist, just as the deeds of Jesus differentiate His words from those of a human prophet. Admittedly, even in this mutually differentiating character, the words and deeds of Jesus do not as such cease to be tokens that can do no more than point toward the Kingdom of God that transcends them. Many heard the words of Jesus and saw His deeds, and yet did not believe in Him. Those, however, who believed in Him did believe in Him on account of His tokens, on account, that is, of His words and deeds.

At the beginning of the life of Jesus stands the miraculous token of His *Virgin Birth*. At the end of His life stands the miraculous token of the *Empty Tomb*. It is precisely to these two miracles that we have to give particular attention. We may, if we will, call the biblical reports of them 'legends'. But let us at least see and understand their meaning as *tokens*! Then we shall no longer discredit them as 'legends', nor shall we be offended by their character as unequivocally miraculous stories, because we shall realize that no stories that were not miraculous could suffice to indicate that to which they point. Both betoken the existence of

Jesus Christ as the human existence which is identical with God Himself, and which thereby, both in its entrance upon and its departure from the human plane, is different from every similar life. Here in the sphere of His creation God Himself, in establishing a new beginning, has condescended to be man. To this the Virgin Birth bears witness. And the Empty Tomb bears witness to the reality of this divine new beginning. It is the unveiling of that which in the new beginning is veiled. But even these tokens can be overlooked. Unbelief is possible despite the fact that we have these miracles, and, it may be, actually in face of these miracles. We may, however, ask whether faith is possible without seeing these tokens and without apprehending them as tokens? Are not they beyond all others the occasion as well as the criterion of faith in the secret of revelation? Is it possible for us to see in Jesus Christ the divine new beginning and the divine triumph if we overlook these tokens and it may be persist in overlooking them completely?

To the tokens of revelation belong in an especial way the existence of the *Prophets* and of the *Apostles*, or, to put it another way, the witness of the Old Testament and the witness of the New. Here too we find both difference and correspondence. The event of revelation has a definite time which precedes it and a definite time which follows it. There is an expectation and there is a recollection of revelation. The subject of both is the same: namely, Jesus Christ—the time fulfilled in the midst of the times. The Prophets and the Apostles are therefore alike also in this respect, that they are men directly called to witness to the Fullness of the times. They belong either to the time which precedes the Fullness of the times, and witness to the future event; or they belong to the time which follows the Fullness of the times, and witness to the past fact. Now of both these are documents; there are prophetic documents belonging to the period of expectation, and there are apostolic documents belonging to the period of recollection. These documents form *Holy Scripture*. Holy Scripture as such is not the revelation. And yet Holy Scripture *is* the revelation, if and in so far as *Jesus Christ* speaks to us through the witness of His prophets and apostles. True, there has never been a single person who for his part could honestly say that he has heard Jesus Christ speak equally clearly in every part and parcel of the Scriptures. Countless people would be obliged in all honesty to admit that there are large portions of Holy Scripture in which they have not yet heard the voice of Jesus Christ. Even the Church, in holding fast to the sacred character or canonicity of *each* and *every* part of the whole of Scripture, only asserts that here within the compass of this Scripture has she at her birth heard Jesus Christ speak; and that here and here only, as far as we know, can Jesus Christ speak to us again. Anyone who should happen to be offended at this 'here only' must first inform us where else Jesus Christ speaks to us. Of course there are many self-appointed witnesses testifying to all sorts of spurious revelations. But are there any other witnesses of the true and unique revelation, any other witnesses of Jesus Christ? Holy Scripture is a *token* of revelation. Unbelief is possible even when confronted by this token. But there has never yet been a faith in the revelation which has passed by this token, a faith which was not rather awakened, nourished and controlled precisely through the instrumentality of *this* token.

Because Holy Scripture exists as a token of revelation, there exist in the Church *Proclamation* (preaching) and *Sacrament* as further tokens of revelation. And here there is repeated in some measure that relation of word and deed which we have found in the life of Jesus. But in the relation between proclamation and sacrament there can also be found reflected the relation between the Old and New Testaments. Preaching is the utterance whose subject and creative form is the biblical witness. As such it is a proclaiming of Jesus Christ's action as present ever anew. The sacrament, on the other hand, is a symbolical act consummated in the sense of, and in accordance with, the biblical witness. It is the confirmation of the action of Jesus as something which has *taken place* for us, and *happened* to us, *once and for all*; of the action which is the source (baptism) and sustenance (Lord's Supper) of our life in faith. Thus preaching and sacrament too are in different ways—but still in this difference at one—mutually explanatory *tokens* of revelation. Neither preaching nor sacrament can be dispensed with; for how should we believe today if the biblical witness also were not re-presented today? Neither preaching nor sacrament can be dispensed with; for surely this re-presentation must consist in testimony to the true revelation as present *as well as* once and for all? Neither preaching nor sacrament, however, is effective of itself in awakening faith today; but both are effective through the power of the revelation which they attest and through that alone.

Because preaching and sacrament exist as tokens of revelation, there also exist in the Church both *congregation* and *ministry*, though again in another connexion and order. The *congregation* exists as the assembly, constituted ever anew, of those who themselves have heard the witness of Holy Scripture through preaching and sacrament, and, through this witness, the proclamation of their election and calling to faith in Jesus Christ, and so have heard the voice of the Good Shepherd

Himself and consequently know that they are responsible for passing on this witness and proclamation pure and unsullied. The *ministry* exists to pass on the Word. This service of passing on the Word is exercised in the name of the congregation of Jesus Christ and therefore by commission from Him. The purpose of such service, like that of the liturgy concerned with the same thing, is to preserve as tokens, in the congregation and for all people, the tokens that have been received. Its purpose, therefore, is to perform the preaching and celebrate the sacraments rightly and diligently; that is, with constant attention to the biblical witness and so in obedience to Jesus Christ. Congregation and ministry are *tokens* of revelation. Their existence and the confession they make are able to awaken faith. How can faith be awakened, if at all, except in and through congregation and ministry? But all the same if faith be awakened it is not congregation and ministry which have done this, but Jesus Christ Himself as the Lord of the congregation and of the ministry.

As a concluding point we come to the individual Christian's *experience* and *exhibition* of *faith*. The actual faith in which man is justified and saved and born again is the hidden work of the Holy Spirit, veiled, indeed completely veiled, by man's own work. For man's own work is and remains the work of a sinner and will always be visible as such.

But here too, the revelation is not without *tokens*. There cannot be faith without *experience*. The hidden faith will, indeed, determine, change and shape the heart and conscience, the desires and the deeds of the sinful man; but certainly not in an unambiguous way, certainly not in such a manner that the believer will be *directly* discernible to himself or to others in his true status as a child of God; but for all that he will be determined, changed and shaped. And this happening, this experience, in its utter insignificance, relativity and infirmity can then, as the reflection of this faith, as the gift of the Holy Spirit, serve (though its evidence is only indirect) to remind him of his faith, and to confirm him in it and so in the revelation which has come to him (*Syllogismus practicus!*). Human experience has no power of its own to become such a reminder or such a confirmation. And that is the error again and again made at this point. Only Jesus Christ can give a man's experience the power to become the visible evidence of the gift of the Holy Spirit, and therefore such a reminder and confirmation. But undoubtedly Jesus Christ both can and does do this. And undoubtedly, in every instance in which a man really believes on Jesus Christ and lives by this faith, he also lives with and by such faith-experiences as *tokens* of revelation now given to *him*. Nor can the faith of the individual Christian exist without showing

71

itself outwardly and to others. As a sinful man, like all other men, the individual Christian stands in their midst and goes in and out amongst them making no boast or claim to be or to have anything special. But since, in virtue of the hidden work of the Holy Spirit, he participates as a believer in something that is indeed special and therefore also in a special experience, his life can signify outwardly and for others something special, can signify an exhibition of faith and so a token of revelation. Of himself he cannot make himself this. He cannot even aim at becoming this. Least of all can he speak of it as something that he is. Nor can he in any case—and here again error is constantly creeping in—adduce his own life as evidence, just where, as witness to Jesus Christ, he is bound to point to Jesus Christ alone. None the less— though happy is the man who knows it not, or, if he knows it, then it is to his own supreme astonishment and even horror!—his own existence can in fact be an evidence for the existence of Jesus Christ. Through Jesus Christ he can, in actual fact, be appointed and placed to be such evidence. But he can never be such evidence in the totality of his life, but only in a definite aspect and a definite function. Even then the revelation will itself be its own proof. This it does, however, by means of *this* token. And we should have to search long for the believer who—in boundless gratitude to Jesus Christ alone—did not owe his faith to this Christ-given token, viz., the exhibition of faith furnished him by other men.

In this whole context, instead of the 'tokens of revelation' we could have spoken of the *Body of Jesus Christ upon earth*, the Body which derives its life and food and drink from His heavenly Body, the humanity of Jesus Christ exalted to the right hand of God. For the earthly Body of Christ is the sum total of the tokens of which we have been speaking. And, since this earthly Body of Christ is again none other than the *Church*, everything we have said about the 'tokens' could also have been said about the Church through which and in which we must be brought together, if we are partakers of the revelation and since we are partakers. The Church is *the* secondary token of revelation—the Church as conditioned by the primary and unconditioned token of the flesh of Jesus Christ, that flesh which the eternal Word has accepted and received into unity with itself. The Church is conditioned and secondary, but none the less, so far as we can see, it is indispensable. At the outset we referred to the sphere and the discipline within which alone the Christian apprehension of revelation can be spoken of. This sphere and discipline are the sphere and the discipline of the Church. Therefore we may ask whether faith in the revelation, and so apprehension of the revelation, is possible, if it is accompanied by disobedience to the *tokens* of revelation or by disregard of them. If this cannot be, then the maxim *extra ecclesiam nulla salus* is still in force and is still valid; *it is something which not even the most profound humility will allow us to deny or qualify.*

III. THE WORK OF REVELATION

Jesus Christ does not merely *point* a way: He *is* the way. Revelation according to Christian apprehension is not merely a matter of communication of divine truth *about* the relation between God and man, a communication which has then to be followed by a corresponding human work—some definite cult or religious and moral line of conduct. It is not a communication of divine truth which has to be *followed* by a corresponding human work in the form of a theological doctrine, at the root of which that communication lay and in which it now attains practical application and theoretical realization. Revelation, as the Christian apprehends it, is certainly such communication of truth. But it is also the work in which God Himself acts in His relation to man—originally in Jesus Christ, mediately in the Church of Jesus Christ. It has therefore been impossible for us to speak of the essence of revelation without straightway speaking also of Reconciliation. The truth revealed

74

to us in revelation is not a doctrine about reconciliation but *is* the reconciliation itself, the reconciling *action* of God. But the human work which is called into being by the revelation can only be the faith by which man beholds the revelation, both in its essence and in its tokens, doing its own work, and in which man lets it do its own work. Thus, since this attitude on man's part signifies and implies the claim laid by God upon his whole life, he accompanies the revelation with service, within the limits of his human capacity.

The revelation, Jesus Christ, is the work in which God Himself *restores* the shattered *order* of the relation between Himself and man. We must always apprehend the revelation as this work of restoration, whether we seek to apprehend it relatively to its essence or its tokens. A shattered relation between God and man has to be restored; hence the work of God, if it is not to consist in abandoning man or in annihilating what He has created, must consist in revelation. Revelation must therefore be revelation—a new event, grace, and therefore judgment upon our confidence that all the potentialities of ordering that relation lie in our own power. Revelation must therefore be God's own existence as man, His entering into our place, our being taken into His. Hence its extraordinary character, a character which more or less attaches also to all tokens of revelation as such.

The *offence* that is everywhere presented to us in revelation does not rest upon divine whim or caprice. The revelation shatters no real order, even though it is in actual fact extraordinary both in its essence and its tokens. Its extraordinary character and its giving offence is due to the fact that in the revelation through God's action, the sheltering of the real order is itself shattered for the purpose of restoring the real order. Paradoxically it is not God who is arbitrary and capricious, but man, man who has shattered the real order, and whom God in His revelation now meets with its restoration.

God Himself is the One who acts. God is the subject in this work. This He is in the life of Jesus Christ Himself. This He is too in the tokens of revelation. Every thought of revelation and every doctrine about it has, according to Christian apprehension, its truth and its importance in the fact, and solely in the fact, that it gives God the glory. And by giving God the glory is meant that these thoughts and doctrines do not concern man, or things, forms, relations, conditions, effects, situations—not even though that relation to God be allowed for! These thoughts and doctrines always refer directly to God as the Lord of this work and therefore as the Lord of man who is the object of this work, and therefore also of the things, forms, relations and the rest, which here are to be taken into account. Christian thought and Christian utterance about revelation revolve continually around the reality of the *sovereignty* of God. Hence Christian thought and Christian utterance involve the recognition, in every event of revelation, of an act of God, and of God as the One who *acts*. Therefore it will never treat the grace of revelation as a supernatural species of matter, but ever anew will seek and find such grace, as an undeserved and unearned miraculous gift, in the free and good will of the Divine *Giver*, the *God* of grace. It will recognize and definitely assert the fact that the revelation takes place in the sphere of God's creation, that is in the sphere of nature and history, in the human sphere. But equally it will recognize that the revelation always takes place through the divine freedom, and therefore also with a spontaneity of its own. The revelation is neither in competition, nor in co-operation with other lords, creators, powers or forces, but is always their Lord and Commander. It is not as if there came through the revelation to man and his world a voice which is man's own. What actually takes place is that God *speaks* and man in his world has to *listen* and to *obey*. It is not as if there were in creation, in nature and history or in the life of man, or in his consciousness thereof, tokens of God's divine revelation ('ordinances of creation') which are simply self-existent. What actually happens is that in His *good pleasure* God establishes such tokens and makes them effective by His own free *dispensation*. In referring to the Church, too, the Christian in his apprehension of revelation will never think of her or speak of her as if God had, so to say, made over His truth and righteousness to the Church herself. The Christian will never think or speak of the Church as if God had transferred His truth and righteousness to her in general, or more particularly to her officials, to be controlled by them. The Christian apprehension will so treat the ecclesiastical authority both in theory and practice that the fact is, and remains, visible that Church authority is no pseudo-divine authority inherent in men, but the authority of the heavenly *Lord* of the Church. The Christian in his apprehension of revelation will never value even Christian experience and Christian work for their own sake. If some experience and some work of the kind does actually appear here and there, he will be grateful for this. But he will recognize without reserve the insignificance and the human frailty of all Christian experience and all Christian work. He will recognize without reserve that in them too sin triumphs. He will not speak as if the aesthetic or moral beauty which they may possess could be identified with righteousness and holiness possessed by them in God's sight. He will not therefore be put out by any aesthetic or moral infirmity which they

78

may have. In that he sees through and beyond the beauty or the lack of beauty that may appear in the lives of those who, though Christians, are and remain creatures, he will never give praise to the creature but always to the Lord and *Creator*.

The work of revelation, as we know it here and now, is, however, the *announcement* of an order re-established. The announcement is as *authentic* as is the fact that God Himself is the subject and the Lord of this work. The announcement is as *sure* and as certain as is the fact that the restoration of order in the relations between God and man has already taken place and is already manifest in the essence of revelation, that is in the existence of Jesus Christ. And yet, in so far as we and the world are concerned, it is the announcement but not yet the accomplishing of this restoration, certain as it is that revelation must be *believed* and *proclaimed* as a work that has taken place once and for all in Jesus Christ. This is as certain as it is that alongside of the time fulfilled and the prophetic time of expectation and the apostolic time of recollection, there is *our* time—the time *before* Abraham and the time *after* the Ascension. This is as certain as it is that we in this time of ours stand in need of the *tokens*, if we are to become and remain contemporaneous with the revelation and if we are to believe—tokens which are not themselves the essence of revelation but only its tokens. Remembering and drawing comfort from the fulfilment which has taken place in Jesus Christ, and accepting that fulfilment as a promise we *await* the fulfilment of our time also. If we ask how for ourselves we share directly in revelation within the sphere of the Church which is the Body of Jesus Christ upon earth, the answer is that, inasmuch as our sharing in the revelation consists in our sharing in the birth and resurrection of Jesus Christ Himself, our sharing is a sharing in *hope*. This sharing can, of course, determine our faith and our life, but it cannot visibly or ultimately transform it. True, the Church can set limits to the State. She can and should remind it of the righteousness and of the judgment of God. But she cannot herself become the State, nor can she make the State into a Church. Theology can, of course, as an ecclesiastical science, perform its definite and necessary service in the sphere of the Church, and in addition it can fulfil the useful function of pointing science to its real and ultimate problem, a problem that still remains unsolved, unelaborated and unconsidered. But it has no systematic correlation or synthesis of human thinking to offer. Theology cannot become philosophy and it cannot permit its task to be usurped by any philosophy. In every generation and amongst all men and people it is possible to secure the proclamation as such of the justification, sanctification and regeneration which takes place in Jesus Christ. But this proclamation cannot allow itself to be changed or transposed into any scheme of life or into any plan for saving men by the solution of political, economic or social problems; and in no circumstances can it be made the proclamation of a Kingdom of God which has already come or has already appeared, even if this be merely in the form of a programme. None of the tokens of revelation is the revelation itself. The revelation, here and now, is Jesus Christ alone. And the work of Jesus Christ, as we know it here and now in the time of divine forbearance is the work of *announcement*. The New Testament ought not, therefore, to surprise us when in more than one passage it employs the conception of 'revelation' as a description of the *Last Things* towards which it sees moving the whole time of forbearance, of tokens and of the Church. In point of fact, the work of revelation, in its full operation upon man and his world, is a future work. But in its full operation it will still be the work of *Jesus Christ*. Consequently our time, even now, is no empty time; it is the time of authentic and sure proclamation and therefore of joyful and confident hope. For our time is the time between the Ascension and the Return of Jesus Christ. It is therefore His time, the time of faith in Him. Accordingly, and in that degree, it is the time of faith in revelation as *already completed*.

III

By the Most Rev. WILLIAM TEMPLE

Archbishop of York

The dominant problem of contemporary religious thought is the problem of revelation. Is there such a thing at all? If there is, what is its mode and form? Is it discoverable in all existing things, or only in some? If in some, then in which, and by what principle are these selected as its vehicle? Where it is found, or believed to be found, what is its authority? Does it convey infallible certainty concerning reality or is it of such a kind as to call for the exercise of reflection and judgment before it is fully apprehended? If it calls for this, are the reflection and the judgment exercised upon it exempt from that liability to error which is otherwise present in all human thought?

A short time back it was commonly said that Materialism was dead; and truly the old fashioned materialism, now distinguished as mechanistic materialism, was dead. In the third quarter of the nineteenth century it looked as if science would

83

increasingly encourage a picture of the world as consisting of atoms, each a hard, indivisible, impenetrable little block, which by their jostlings and combinations gave rise to all the varieties of existence, not excluding thought. But before the century had ended there were signs of a reaction within the world of science itself; and since the beginning of the twentieth century a new situation has arisen which is philosophically very different from what had preceded it, but contains for religious thought problems no less acute and urgent.

Men of science in ever greater numbers assure us of their conviction that the world, as they study it, seems more like a thought than like a machine. But the thought which they find it to resemble is mathematical thought. There is so far nothing to encourage the attribution of moral attributes to this thought. The heavens declare the mathematical accuracy of God, and the firmament sheweth His geometrical mastery; but that is all of glory or handywork that science can find there. We need not be dismayed at this, for physical science is not concerned with moral questions, and no science, as the word is now understood, is concerned with ultimate explanations; there is no occasion for alarm in the fact that science has not found what it never sought. But the deliverances of science have provided a context in which the two most characteristic tendencies in contemporary thought find a congruous, and even comfortable, setting.

One of these is no novelty. It is the familiar interpretation of the universe by means of spiritual conceptions which, however, leaves no room for specific revelation. This view of the world seeks to justify man's religious impulses and aspirations by correlating them with an ultimate spiritual principle in which the existence and process of the universe are grounded. To this is often given the name of God; and God, as so conceived, has some of the chief attributes which adherents of the great positive religions usually believe to be His. All the world proceeds from Him: in all of it, therefore, He is revealed. It is indeed His glory that the heavens declare and His handiwork that the firmament sheweth. History also discloses His purpose, and in its course His judgments may be traced, in the sense that the laws governing its sequence and therefore determining its episodes are His laws. But while it is thus insisted that He does everything in general, it is with equal emphasis denied that He does anything in particular.

Such a view is compatible with a certain exercise of man's religious propensities. But it is not compatible with Christianity. For Christianity is committed irretrievably to two convictions: first, that God has a definite purpose for the world which He is accomplishing partly, though not wholly, in the arena of human history; and secondly, that He has not only revealed His character, but has Himself taken personal action, in Jesus of Nazareth, who is Himself the decisive fact in history and the agent for the accomplishment therein of the divine purpose.

The other view of the world characteristic of our time is a revival of materialism with a significant modification. It is the Dialectical Materialism of Marx, Engels, and Lenin. As the former is the view to which the influences of physical science have inclined those sections of society which, being tolerably comfortable, seek progress but not revolution, so this is the view to which the same influences have inclined those sections which find themselves shut out from what would seem to them their fair share of the fruits of a scientific civilization, and despair of accomplishing by gradual development the transformation of society which they desire. According to this view, Mind and Matter are both realities; or (if that mode of expression be preferred) reality has two distinguishable modes of activity, of which one is studied in the physical sciences, and one in the mental sciences. These two groups of sciences rightly employ different categories. Through the clash of mind and matter, each acting in its own fashion, the movement of history results. But mind is here conceived as always reacting, according to its own laws, to the situation presented by its material environment. So, of course, in the physical sciences it does. The physicist or the chemist must not import into his study preconceived notions of how natural forces ought to behave; he must observe their actual behaviour and use his mental processes only to classify and correlate what he thus observes. In the same way the Dialectical Materialist maintains that the mind of a statesman or of a man of business can only deal, by its own fixed laws, with the material situation confronting him. He cannot start with conceptions or aspirations due to the nature of Mind or Spirit and impose these upon his environment. Matter has therefore, always the initiative; progress never comes by the spiritual influence of a seer whose vision kindles such ardour in his followers that they reshape the world in accordance with their dream; progress only comes, but inevitably comes, by the pressure of material facts creating a situation to which sufficient minds react in determination to change the system. Instead of trusting to a growth of the spirit of love in men's hearts till it fashions an actual partnership of goods, the Dialectical Materialist awaits the time when pressure of events creates the partnership of goods, and trusts to this to develop the answering spirit of love.

In this, as in the former view, there is much
which must be recognized as true and congruous
with Christianity. It is true that man's mind or
spirit can deal only with facts as it finds them.
Nothing is so futile as to attempt to impose upon
them a mould which they are not fitted to receive.
And the Dialectical Materialist will, nine times
out of ten, be right in his account of such senti-
mental reformism. The love which prompts it
may be real, but it is shallow; at bottom self is the
central principle; the effort is not to serve the
world, but to impose 'my' notions upon it. True
love, being free from self-centredness, has the
humility to study the facts as they are and adapt
its policy to them, though the goal of its policy is
set by its own nature and not dictated by the
external facts. For this reason the true Christian
is always realistic, and often seems even cynical to
sentimentalists whose chief desire is not to serve
their neighbours, but to have the pleasure of
exercising their own kindly disposition.

Now both these views—the *bourgeois* pantheist
and the revolutionary Dialectical Materialist—are
rooted in an initial and often unconscious conviction that the last term in the explanation of Reality
is Truth as the intellect apprehends it, or Intellect
as apprehension of Truth; in other words, the last
term is itself static, and is such as to generate no
movement—Reality on one side, contemplation

88

on the other. The Reality may be a process, as, for Dialectical Materialism, it is, but for this view no less than for Pantheism or Absolute Idealism, Purpose is irrelevant in the last resort. There are particular purposes, of course; they are parts of the process, in which Ultimate Reality manifests itself, or through which the clash of matter and mind keeps the process moving. But they are only episodes. Purpose is not, in either of these views, characteristic of reality as a whole.

This is the familiar Greek view, both Platonic and Aristotelian, though it is more completely characteristic of Aristotle than of Plato. Both of the chief contemporary currents of thought are particular modes of it. It is directly opposed to the Hebraic or biblical view which finds the explanation of the world in a Divine Will active in creation and in the providential control of history, and demanding of men active submission to itself, and cooperation in the fulfilment of its purposes. It would not be appropriate here to discuss the two views from the philosophical standpoint;[1] but it is most relevant to our purpose to insist that the Christian Religion is irretrievably committed to the biblical doctrine of the living God, and to notice what are its chief consequences.

[1] I have tried to establish the philosophical superiority of the biblical view in my recent Gifford Lectures—*Nature, Man and God* (Macmillan).

It has been pointed out that the contrast often drawn between East and West only applies to those geographical areas in modern times. The atmosphere of Eastern thought and custom is not very different from that of Mediterranean culture in the six centuries between 400 B.C. and A.D. 200. There was the same bewildering combination of lofty philosophical speculation with immoral cults, the same failure of the accepted religions to provide ethical impulse. And wherever Ultimate Reality is so conceived as to make our appropriate attitude towards it a contemplative absorption, or absorbed contemplation, this must always be so. Only where the Ultimate Reality is known as Righteous Will can religious devotion become a source of ethical inspiration. But where that is so, knowledge of God and recognition of a duty of obedience to God become inseparable, for He is known, not as a thing, but as a personal Creator and Lord. This conception of God is given to us through the Bible and scarcely appears except under the influence of the Bible. For though it may be found here and there outside the range of that influence, as for example in Zoroaster, these flashes of illumination remain isolated, and give rise to no abiding and deepening tradition of faith. The conviction that the Ultimate Reality is Righteous Will, with the corollary that for man the only truth, or correspondence with reality, is obedience—this is due to that series of events and experiences of which the Bible is the record.

Before going further it may be well to forestall a difficulty which easily presents itself at this point. In some parts of the Old Testament God is represented as willing events in nature or actions on the part of men which it is hard to regard as being desired by One whose eternal nature is made manifest in Jesus Christ. For some this difficulty is increased by what may be called the Tolstoyan apprehension of Christ. The central figure of the Gospel story is not adequately described by the adjectives 'meek and gentle', and illustrates one aspect of the Kingdom of God by sayings such as this: 'The king was wroth; and he sent his armies, and destroyed those murderers, and burned their city.' But when all is said, it cannot be denied that the picture of Jehovah in some parts of the Old Testament is incompatible with that of the Father concerning whom our Lord is recorded as saying: 'He that hath seen me hath seen the Father.' This fact presents no serious problem to those who accept the view of revelation set forth in this essay. For the record is not itself the revelation; it is the record, set down by men in the illumination supplied by their knowledge of God, of the facts wherein the revelation was given. Defects in their knowledge of God must therefore affect and in some instances deflect

91

the record; so that revelation could not be complete until the Eternal Word of God Himself 'became flesh and tabernacled among us', displaying to those whose hearts were attuned by the Divine Spirit to His message 'the glory as of an only begotten from a father'.[1] Consequently, in the words of the Anglican Bishops at the Lambeth Conference of 1930—'As Jesus Christ is the crown, so also is He the criterion of all revelation. We would impress upon Christian people the necessity of banishing from their minds ideas concerning the character of God which are inconsistent with the character of Jesus Christ.'[2]

The progressive character of the biblical revelation of the divine nature and of the righteousness of the divine will in no way diminishes the clear witness of the Bible to that divine will as the governing power in nature and in history, or to Righteous Will as the aspect of the divine nature most relevant to human faith, worship and conduct.

It is a characteristic of Will as known in ourselves that it maintains and exhibits its own constancy in a series of choices each adapted to the circumstances with which it deals. It is distinguished from a mechanical object by this peculiarity. A mechanical object acts in identically the same way whenever the same mechanical forces

[1] St. John i. 14.

[2] *Report of the Lambeth Conference*, 1930, p. 39.

play upon it. The will may respond to identical suggestions in totally different ways at different times, so that, whatever the circumstances, it may steadfastly pursue the accomplishment of its purpose. The wise administrator adapts his action on different occasions to the capacity and temper of each of those with whom or through whom he must act. He does not behave with mechanical uniformity. He is reliable, not in the sense of always doing again what he did before, but in the sense of always doing what is wise and conducive to the success of his policy. To suppose that God is constant in any other sense than this, and to attribute to Him an invariable uniformity of action, is to deny personality to Him and to treat Him as a thing—an intellectual principle or a universally diffused substance, but not a Person or Being characterized by Will.

In the series of choices wherein any Will expresses itself some are normal and commonplace, others are special and revealing. The great man and the ordinary citizen may eat and drink and sleep by the same rules; it is when an emergency arises that they reveal the difference between them. Then the great man acts with a mastery of circumstance; the small man, finding his routine inapplicable, succumbs to helplessness. Two brothers may have grown up together, sharing the same home, the same interests, the same influences; apparently they are indistinguishable in character; then suddenly they are confronted with great danger; one shows courage, the other cowardice. Very often in such circumstances the friends of the former will say: 'I never knew he had it in him.' They recognize that his courageous action is a revelation of his real character. He did not then become brave for the first time. But he then showed for the first time how brave he was. And if there had been no emergency he would not have showed it at all.

Wherever there is Will or Personality, there must be this distinction between normal and revelatory actions. The normal actions show character in some degree, but its true depth is only shown when special circumstances call for special response. So, if God is to be known as Person or Will, this must mean that He too acts normally in ways adapted to the fulfilment of His purpose in general, but acts in special, and therefore specially revealing, ways when emergency makes this fitting; and He is only known fully to those who know Him in these specially revealing acts. To suppose that God can be known by a general inference from observed nature or history, apart from the special acts wherein He is specially revealed, is once again to deny His personality and to treat Him as a thing, which has no capacity to adjust its reaction to varying needs.

94

Now, if it be God, the Ultimate Reality, who is revealed, then all things must in some measure reveal Him. A special revelation which bore no relation to the general nature of the universe and of history, could not be a revelation of God. There can only be a special revelation of God if the Ultimate Reality is personal; for only personality can be the source of such special revelation, which must be an act of Will; while if the special revelation discloses anything other or less than the Ultimate Reality, it is not a revelation of God. On the other hand, if God is personal, there must be general revelation of His attributes in all that exists, for all is His creation, and there must also be special revelation of His character in distinctive actions called forth by the emergencies of history. The belief in Divine Personality and the belief in specific Revelation go together; each necessitates the other.

The Bible affirms both in indissoluble unity. It is the record of the revealing acts of God. Sometimes it has been spoken of as the record of a particular religious experience, enjoyed by a certain national community, the members of that community who were loyal to its tradition entering ever more deeply into the meaning of that experience. Those who so conceive it tend to take the prophetic consciousness as the central point in which the event of revelation takes place. And so the prophet comes to be regarded as the primary vehicle of revelation. But this is not the account which the Bible gives of itself. No doubt it is such a record of the religious experience of Israel; but this is not its predominant characteristic. First and foremost it is the record of those historic facts, which were themselves the occasion of the experience of Israel, prophets and people alike. It is not the subjective consciousness of the prophets which is primary; it is the facts of which they were conscious—the Exodus, the division of the Kingdom, the rise of Assyria and Babylon, the retreat of Sennacherib, the Captivity and the Exile, the Return of the Remnant, the rebuilding of the Temple, the triumph of the Maccabees. It is here, in these great facts, that the Lord made bare His arm, and the prophetic consciousness is first and foremost a consciousness of these facts as mighty acts of God.

'Of God'—and therefore of the Creator of the world, in which, as His handiwork, His nature is in part revealed. Once more, before leaving it as a matter firmly settled, we reiterate this most important point. 'Unless all existence is a medium of Revelation, no particular Revelation is possible; for the possibility of Revelation depends on the personal quality of that supreme and Ultimate Reality which is God. If there is no Ultimate Reality, which is the ground of all else, then there is no God to be revealed; if that Reality is not personal, there can be no special Revelation but only uniform procedure; if there be an Ultimate Reality, and this is personal, then all existence is Revelation. Either all occurrences are in some degree revelation of God, or else there is no such revelation at all; for the conditions of the possibility of any revelation require that there should be nothing which is not revelation. Only if God is revealed in the rising of the sun in the sky can He be revealed in the rising of a son of man from the dead; only if He is revealed in the history of Syrians and Philistines can He be revealed in the history of Israel;[1] only if He chooses all men for His own can He choose any at all; only if nothing is profane can anything be sacred. It is necessary to stress with all possible emphasis this universal quality of revelation in general before going on to discuss the various modes of particular revelation; for the latter, if detached from the former, loses its root in the rational coherence of the world and consequently becomes itself a superstition and a fruitful source of superstitions. But if all existence is a revelation of God, as it must be if He is the ground of its existence, and if the God thus revealed is personal, then there is more ground in reason for expecting particular revelations than for denying them.'[2]

[1] See Amos ix. 7.

[2] This paragraph is quoted from the author's *Nature, Man and God*, pp. 306-307.

This point is, no doubt, open to misunderstanding. What is contended is that in all creation some revelation of God is offered; but for two reasons it may not be effectually received. The first reason is that, if we seek the revelation of God in nature and in history, we can only hope to find it with any security when the drama of history is played out to the end; any isolated episode or period may be so misleading in its suggestion as to be a source of falsehood rather than of truth. The second reason is that our minds are clouded by sin, so that we have not any sure means of estimating truly the values of natural processes or historical events. We are not indeed without some basis for judgment; unless our apprehension of good and evil is in principle reliable, no revelation can assist us, for we could not recognize it. But our application of the principle is rendered highly precarious by the distortion of perspective which is a result of our self-centredness, so that our interpretation of the diffused revelation offered in nature and in history is unreliable unless it is established by some special and positive revelation wherein the divine nature and character are manifested as the diffused rays of sunlight are gathered in the focus of a burning-glass.

It is true, no doubt, that this difficulty also arises in connexion with our reception of, and response to, a special revelation. For, here too, our capacity for spiritual appreciation is a variable factor. In the ordinary sense of the words it is simply not true that

We needs must love the highest when we see it.

If our sensitiveness is insufficiently developed, we dislike it very much. The Fourth Gospel attributes to our Lord the words: 'Now have they both seen and hated both me and my Father.' But our capacity for appreciation is actually developed by the influence of objects worthy of admiration; and one test of a true revelation is its capacity to call forth in ever increasing measure the awareness of its divine character, and the resultant submission to its sway of our conscience, heart and will. The course of nature and history can never be so fully apprehended by finite and sinful man as to call forth this response whereby alone the distinctive quality of revelation is recognized. That can only be done by a particular and specific act of revelation.

Most positive religions insist upon such particular revelations. The Christian will readily believe that each of these is a real revelation; but all with one exception he will regard as partial, not complete, revelations, which if taken as complete become the source of superstition and error. But adherents of those religions may reasonably demand to know the criterion by which Christians claim superiority and indeed complete-

99

75071

ness for the Revelation which they have themselves
received. This demand may best be met by a
consideration of the special characteristics of that
revelation and the extent to which these include
in a fuller form the qualities found in other particular revelations, and also by enquiring how far
the Christian revelation surpasses others in pro-
viding the source of a fully satisfactory philosophy
of life and of the universe. It is clear that the scope
of a short essay is insufficient for a discussion of
these themes, but an indication must be offered of
the direction which such a discussion must follow.

All human experience contains two factors, the
subjective and the objective. Revelation must of
necessity conform to this rule. But what is the
nature of the 'object' in which the revelation is
offered? Is it a Truth?—that is to say something
primarily belonging to the 'subject' though having
application to the 'object' world. Or to put the
question in another way, does God chiefly give
His revelation by introducing ideas—whether
convictions or determinations—into the mind of
the prophet, or by guiding external events in
which the prophet sees His hand? The question
is of great practical importance for religion. For
if God chiefly follows the way of introducing
ideas, then revelation itself can be formulated in
propositions which are indubitably true. But if He
chiefly follows the way of guiding external events,

these constitute the primary vehicle of the revelation; and events cannot be fully formulated in propositions; the event is always richer than any description of it.

Under the influence of that exaggerated intellectualism which Christian Theology inherited from Greek Philosophy, a theory of revelation has usually been accepted in the Christian Church which fits very ill with the actual revelation treasured by the Church. For the common theory has been that through revelation we receive divinely guaranteed Truths. To this view there are two serious objections; one is that any such introduction of guaranteed Truth into the mind has no analogy in the rest of our experience. That alone would not be a fatal objection, because it might well be claimed that divine revelation, if it occurs, may well be unique and without analogue; and this claim would be no more than partly met by the recollection that if there is to be special revelation in any occurrences there must be general revelation in all occurrences. But the memory of this principle will incline us to prefer a view which avoids so complete a distinction and separation of specific revelation from all other experience.

The other objection to the traditional view is far more serious. It consists in the fact that the Bible, accepted as the repository of revelation, consists to so small an extent of the kind of Truths in question. Christians have had recourse to various devices at different times in order to fit the accepted theory of revelation to the actual revelation received. One of the earliest was the device of allegorical interpretation. The whole Bible is true, it was held, but what it means is not always what it seems to say. Thus St. Augustine had no more belief in six 'days' of creation, understood as periods of time, than any modern believer in evolution; the successive days are, according to him, a figure for the successive stages in which finite intelligences could apprehend the divine activity of creation, which in itself he held to be one and indivisible. But if the guaranteed truth is not the obvious meaning of the words, and the spiritual fruit (be it good or bad) of guaranteed truth is to be garnered, there must be an interpreter equally guaranteed. So, by this road, men are forced back from the infallible Book to the infallible Church and to the infallible Spokesman of that Church. In order to escape from this, some have attached the divine guarantee to the actual statements contained in the Bible when literally understood. Because they accept the Bible as the Word of God, they regard themselves as pledged to believe and to teach that the world was created out of nothing in a week, or that strange astronomical occurrences took place in connexion with the battle of Bethhoron; and whenever it appears that there is some way of showing that what is asserted really may have occurred, it is supposed that faith has received a new support.

It was not in this way that Luther and the other great reformers understood the Bible as the Word of God when they recalled men to it as the one rule of faith. For them the Word of God was a living, present utterance of the living God to the souls of men, spoken through, rather than contained in, the printed Bible, and its divine quality was vindicated by the 'testimony of the Holy Spirit' in the heart and conscience of the reader. This is a view of Scripture precisely congruous with the contents of Scripture. For when we turn to these, what do we find? There are very few propositions suitable to be made the subject matter of religious faith. One of these is indeed of supreme importance. The great declaration 'The LORD our God, the LORD is one'[1] dominates the entire Bible. But we must not overlook the fact that it is offered as a ground for a law of worship, and that it is rather an inevitable apprehension arising from truly directed worship and obedience than an independent theological proposition given and accepted in detachment from that experience.

Broadly speaking, as has been said, the Bible is a record of events as these were seen by men who observed them in the illumination of faith in God.

[1]Deuteronomy vi. 4.

The prophets, in whom the 'subjective' element—the human apprehension of the revelation, reaches its culmination, do not appeal chiefly to their inner certainty that God has spoken to their hearts, though this is not unknown;[1] they appeal chiefly to the great events of past or present, especially the Exodus. It is of little importance how much of the record of that event represents the play of imagination stimulated by memory of the great deliverance; but it is of great importance that behind all prophetic confidence in face of menaces which threaten overwhelming disaster there is the assurance of a deliverance actually wrought.

This complete objectivity of the revelation finds its completest illustration in the Incarnation. Against all suggestions that the fact is indifferent, that the human nature of Christ may have been a mere phantasm, or (to take a modern counterpart) that only the truth of the idea is important, St. John urgently insists on the central importance of the fact that 'Jesus Christ is come in the flesh'. The revelation is not a doctrine or a system of theology or a code of ethics or a way of life; it is a Life actually lived, culminating in actual Death and actual Resurrection, upon the plane of history. It all took place in a particular country, Palestine, and at a particular date, 'under Pontius Pilate'.

It is hard to exaggerate the importance of this

[1] *E.g.* Jeremiah xxiii. 18, 22.

point. Much of the difficulty that men find in accepting traditional Christianity is due to their belief that what is chiefly asked of them is intellectual assent to certain propositions. They may not regard these as untrue, but they refuse to affirm them until they have worked them out for themselves; they see no sufficient reason for taking them on trust. In revolt against what seems to them an exaggeration of formalism they desire a 'formless faith', though they often agree, when challenged, that this would be hard to transmit from generation to generation or to propagate through the world. But if the revelation is given in events, and supremely in the historical Person of Christ, this difficulty is avoided. For an event is not vague or indefinite, even if no number of theories exhaust its significance, and men who differ profoundly in their theories of the Atonement may kneel together in penitence and gratitude at the foot of the cross. 'Faith is not the holding of correct doctrines, but personal fellowship with the living God. Correct doctrine will both express this, assist it and issue from it; incorrect doctrine will misrepresent this and hinder or prevent it. Doctrine is of an importance too great to be exaggerated, but its place is secondary, not primary. I do not believe in any creed, but I use certain creeds to express, to conserve, and to deepen my belief in God. What is offered to man's apprehension in any specific revelation is not truth concerning God but the living God Himself.'[1]

It is perhaps worth while to remark here in passing that the report on 'The Church's Common Confession of Faith' which was received by the first World Conference on Faith and Order, held at Lausanne in 1927, did not offer an actual creed either ancient or modern for universal acceptance, but declared that 'notwithstanding the differences in doctrine among us, we are united in a common Christian Faith, which is proclaimed in the Holy Scriptures and is witnessed to and safeguarded in the Oecumenical Creed, commonly called the Nicene, and in the Apostles' Creed, which Faith is continuously confirmed in the spiritual experience of the Church of Christ.'[2]

That puts it exactly right. The faith of a Christian is not set upon the creeds, nor even fully expressed in the creeds; but the creeds bear witness to it and safeguard it. That faith itself is set upon God and is truly expressed only in the whole of life—which includes of course the life of the mind, but is not limited to this. Such faith is our response to the revelation objectively given in the historical Person, Jesus Christ.

But if the objectivity of the actual revelation is here at its height, so is the requirement of subjec-

---

[1] Quoted from *Nature, Man and God*, p. 322.
[2] *Faith and Order*, p. 466.

tive appreciation. Of the many who heard the words and saw the deeds of Christ, only some 'beheld his glory, glory as of an only begotten from a father'. That light which shone through His human nature from the Father in heaven could not be perceived by all. The eyes of their minds were not sensitive to its rays. Thus the coming of Christ, though its purpose is salvation, issues in judgment; 'And this is the judgement, that the light is come into the world, and men loved the darkness rather than the light.'

In order that the revelation may effectively reveal or disclose the Divine Purpose there must be men attuned to it so as to discern and in part understand it. The Apostles were necessary to the effectual disclosure of the Divine Nature which the Incarnation was designed to offer. If none had 'beheld His glory' it would still have been there; the Life and the Death and the Resurrection are in themselves the manifestation of God in the flesh. But though the manifestation would have occurred, it would have been sterile unless some could apprehend it. So it had been with the prophets. If none had been able to interpret the mighty acts of God as what they were, they would have been wrought partly in vain. The essential condition of effectual revelation is the coincidence of divinely controlled event and minds divinely illumined to read it aright.

Consequently in effective revelation two factors must normally be present, the objective event and the mind qualified to interpret it; but behind each is the purposive action of the Living God. It is important to realize that revelation does not in the least depend for its quality on our capacity or incapacity to trace the manner of control exercised by the divine will over either the event or the mind which interprets it. The possibility of what are called miracles is involved in the very idea of revelation; for, as we saw, this implies a Deity Who is constant, not mechanically but in purpose, and may therefore manifest His constancy in adjustments of His action to the facts of the moment in any degree that the fulfilment of His purpose demands. As Christ very plainly taught, we should see God at work in the regular processes of nature—the rising of the sun, the falling of the rain, the growth of the seed till harvest—no less than in what seem to be unpredictable occurrences. If God exists He governs all things; and to 'explain' scientifically an event in which men have seen Him evidently at work is not to deny His activity in that event, but only to learn what was the mode of His activity. The retreat of Sennacherib's army from Jerusalem was no doubt due to a pestilence breaking out in the main army which was in the neighbourhood of Egypt; but that does not in the least invalidate Isaiah's interpretation of it—'I will put my hook in thy nose'. As we look back we can see that the preservation of the little hill fortress of Jerusalem was much more important than any conflict between the 'Great Powers'—Egypt and Assyria. It really made no serious difference to the world which of them might gain advantage over the other. But if, as Isaiah held, the faith of Judah in the one Living and Righteous God was at that date bound up with His sanctuary on Mount Sion, it was of high importance to the divine purpose that Sion should be inviolate. The pestilence, like the Assyrian Empire itself, was a rod in God's hand. A century later it would be different; those who had learnt the prophetic faith would be independent of its local expression, and would even be strengthened in their hold upon it by having to dispense with such aids and throw themselves back upon God when all earthly hopes and ambitions were destroyed. At that time the same divine purpose which once required the preservation of Jerusalem would require its destruction, and Jeremiah would be as true a prophet in announcing this as Isaiah in announcing the inviolability of the sanctuary. And in the Exile, Josiah's reforms which were too late to avert the catastrophe would bear fruit in preserving the Remnant who would return to supply the hearts capable of welcoming Messiah at His coming.

As the event in which the divine purpose can be traced keeps its full quality of revelation however much it be 'explained' by scientific enquiry, so the illumination of mind whereby the event is interpreted is none the less due to the divine Spirit even though it appears that He makes use of normal psychological processes to produce it. Such an understanding of God's purpose for their people and times as the prophets displayed was due to a communion of their spirits with the Spirit of God. But He did not come upon souls totally unprepared and insert His message by some process of hypnotic suggestion. He had Himself prepared them by the history which He had guided, and by earlier prophets interpreting that history. The prophet seldom regards himself as saying something essentially new, though we, looking back, can often see its novelty; the prophet feels himself to be recalling the people to loyalty to an earlier and purer faith, to obedience to the Law given through Moses, to trust in the God who called and guided Abraham. So the divinely guided history trains the minds which are by divine appointment to trace in that history the movement of the divine purpose.

That has been true, no doubt, of other traditions than that of Israel. That, so far as it goes, is rather testimony to the authenticity of the biblical revelation than the reverse. If God is God indeed, then

He is Lord not of Israel only, but of all nations; and we shall expect that if we find His method of disclosing Himself to men, we shall also find that it is of general application. But there is a difference. I well remember as a schoolboy asking my father if Plato was not as truly inspired as Isaiah, and his answering 'Yes, but Plato did not know he was inspired and Isaiah did'. This is the distinctive fact about Israel—not that God cared only for this nation, but that He led them to know that they were cared for by a God Who was not their God only—to know that they were in the hands of the God of all the earth. So from before the dawn of exact history we find in the world a community conscious of divine commission; if Abraham is the name for a tribe in migration, that only underlines the fact thus stated. Within this community those who live by obedience to God as known to them become able to know more and to interpret more profoundly the events which disclose and set forward His purpose. The sense of commission takes the form of an obligation not only to obey, but to bear witness before other nations. To Israel alone has been given the knowledge of God, the Ultimate Reality, as Living and Righteous Will, to Whom we conform ourselves not only by accurate thought as seekers for truth, nor only by concentrated contemplation as lovers of beauty, but by the obedience to the moral law as responsible persons. For this reason 'Salvation is from the Jews', and if the crises in the history of this community are recorded as marked by those 'miraculous' events which are specially self-revealing acts of God, we can easily see the reason for such differentiation. But salvation must proceed from them and not remain with them, confined to their national tradition; the servant of the Lord is not only to 'raise up the tribes of Jacob, and to restore the preserved of Israel'; God gives him also 'for a light to the Gentiles, that my salvation may be unto the end of the earth'.[1]

It was only a portion of Israel after the flesh that could respond to the call or discharge the commission—only the Remnant of which the prophets speak. And when the Messiah came, even this Remnant failed. Through the debris of a shattered formalism, into which the faith of Israel had been petrified, the Messiah would dig down to the faith that could penetrate His disguise and recognize Him for what He was, and on this rock, found in Simon Bar-Jonas, He would build once more the Church of the Living God, the commissioned community. Yet that faith was still insecure. Even in the moment of its new illumination 'Peter took him, and began to rebuke him'. When the crisis came 'all the disciples forsook him, and fled'. Going forth alone, offering His sacrifice alone, dying alone, bursting death's bonds

[1] Isaiah xlix. 6.

alone—in all this He is alone in His own Person the Israel of God; the faithful Remnant, the Servant of the Lord, is one only, Jesus the Messiah. But in Him the community is reconstituted; the apostolic band, rallied by His Resurrection, again comes together; it is filled with the Spirit; to it are joined those ready to respond and marked for salvation; and all these find themselves to be 'in the Messiah', to be as various limbs in His Body, to be, despite all differences, 'one man in Messiah Jesus'.

So the Christian Church, the new Israel, is inaugurated. It is constituted by the Incarnate Word of God, the Word spoken in Jesus of Nazareth; and it is itself a part of that Word which constitutes it. For the Living Word of God is the knowledge of God given to the commissioned community, and the fellowship of believers is not merely the congregation to which the Word is proclaimed, but is, in virtue of its nature as fellowship, a proclamation of that Word. For here is that 'new creation' wherein tensions and conflicts are abolished, and where not rivalry but reconciliation is the law of life.[1] So far as Christians live 'worthily of the calling wherewith they are called' they exhibit a fellowship transcending all divisions, and therein proclaim to the distracted world that word of reconciliation which found its perfect utterance in the obedience of Christ. The world will believe

[1] II Corinthians v. 17, 19.

that Christ is its Saviour when it sees Christians actually saved by Him from the evils that afflict it. We too, if we are Christians, are in Christ, members of His Body, citizens of the commissioned community and therefore called to be the channels and vehicles of revelation.

The whole reality of this revelation finds its perfect and focal expression in Jesus Himself. It is of supreme importance that it should thus be given in a Person. It is of supreme importance that He wrote no book. It is even of greater advantage that there is no single deed or saying of which we can be perfectly sure that He said or did precisely this or that. Indeed of His sayings we have no exact reproduction, for presumably He spoke in Aramaic, and our records are in Greek, and all translation makes some difference. But the revelation is not in His teaching nor in His acts; it is Himself. The records which we have bring us nearer to Himself than would a series of photographs and phonographic records; for persons are known in personal relationships and what we have is the record of such relationships as illustrated by the impression which He made on a variety of persons in a series of revealing moments. It is not necessarily those who spend most time with a man who know him best; it may happen that they see only the routine which governs the fabric of his life; those who are in his company only for a moment, but that a critical moment calling for exercise of all his qualities, may see a reality not disclosed in daily routine. The episodes selected for record in the Gospels are not very many; but they are revealing. We can have about Napoleon far more numerous distinct pieces of information than we have about Jesus of Nazareth; but we do not personally know Napoleon as we can know Him, even if it be only 'knowledge after the flesh' that is in our minds, and no thought of spiritual communion with Him as ever present Lord.

There are two forms of universality in the apprehension or presentation of truth. One is the scientific grasp of 'laws' or principles invariably illustrated by the behaviour of those objects to which they apply. These have to become more general as the sphere of their application is enlarged, till at last, when true universality is reached, no law can be formulated except the Principle of Sufficient Reason. The other form of universality is the artistic, where universality is achieved through individualization. The psychologist analyses an emotion, such as jealousy, and can tell us what are its component parts; then, after one fashion, we 'understand' a jealous man. The dramatist exhibits before our eyes Othello, 'perplext in the extreme', and after another fashion we understand all jealous men. The dramatic type fails in proportion as it is a type only; it succeeds in so far as it is a truly individual instance of the type. So with the Universality of Christ: because the authority to which we submit is a Person, not a code of rules, there is no conceivable set of circumstances in which loyalty to Him will not control us or the love of Christ constrain us; because He never legislated, He can be a source of direction for every phase of civilization; because all His utterances are strictly occasional, every one is of universal import.

We are thus led to consider the comparative claims of this revelation and other supposed special revelations. Only one is of at all the same type; for though in the great religions of the East there are sacred writings, and for some of these a claim to inspiration has been advanced not less in principle than the claim which Jews and Christians have made for their Scriptures, yet the cause of religion is not regarded as damaged by an admission that the stories narrated in those sacred books are legendary and no more. For all emphasis is laid on truth of idea, and whatever imparts to the mind true ideas is, for those religions, adequate revelation. Thus revelation actually takes place on one side only of the relation between subject and object in experience; it is found in the mind or spirit of man, not in the external event. This of course coheres with the characteristic Eastern philosophy which regards the material world as illusory, and seeks to spiritualize experience by denying its material properties. This refusal of recognition to matter inevitably results in a failure to bring the material aspects of life under spiritual control; and as most historical movements largely concern material things, it is hard for a religion which achieves spirituality by turning its back on matter to dominate historical movements. The present nationalist ferment in India, China and Japan can hope for little of stimulus, or of check, or of purification from the religions traditional in those countries. Confucianism is, indeed, of a different type, being rather an ethical and social tradition than a religion as that word is commonly understood. It is embodied in custom, and in the teaching which prescribes custom, and is therefore limited to circumstances where that custom is applicable.

In Islam a claim is made for a revelation in the Koran similar at first sight to that found in the Bible, and Mohammed is regarded by his followers with a veneration greater than that paid by Jews or Christians to any prophet. But he is still the Prophet and no more; the revelation is in his message, not in himself; it is therefore still only on the subjective side of the subject-object relation. Moreover it mainly consists of precepts and the requirement is of obedience to a law rather than of loyalty and love to a Person.

In short, the revelation which constitutes other great religions is embodied either in precepts or in customs; and for this reason the other great religions have been purely conservative forces tending to stereotype the civilization in which they took their origin, because only in those circumstances can the precepts be precisely obeyed, or the customs punctually followed. This influence has combined with the natural tendency of all natural religion to conservatism; for religion is largely a matter of feeling, and feeling is stirred chiefly by association, so that religion is most easily fostered by what is intimately familiar—the prayers learnt at a mother's knee, and the hymn with its tune, however deplorable, which has been known since childhood.

This tendency is inherent in all natural religion; but whereas the other great religions confirm it, the Gospel corrects it. In the perpetual recurrence of attention to the one theme of the Lord's Birth, Life, Death, and Resurrection there is provided the familiarity which by old association evokes strength of feeling; but in the effort to subject all life to His spirit there is a spring of perpetual progress. He gave no precepts except that we should love one another; that precept can be obeyed in all human circumstances and relationships, but the actions which it will prompt may be indefinitely various. Loyalty to a Person is a spring of conduct more universal in its relevance than any rule of conduct can ever be; it covers all life; the Spirit by which we are to live is more exacting than any 'letter'. It must in honesty be recognized that the Christian Church, as a historically organized society, has been by no means constant in living up to this principle. It has often presented itself as a reactionary force. This is because Christianity is, among other things, a religion. It is not first and foremost a religion. It is first and foremost a Gospel, and secondly a faith responsive to that Gospel. But this faith expresses itself in part as a religion, and this exposes Christians to the temptations incident to all human religion. Often, and in disastrous measure, they— let me say rather we—have yielded to those temptations. For love of our old religious habits we have refused 'the call upwards which God gives in Christ Jesus'.[1] But so far as this has happened we have been bad Christians. For the essence of the Christian life is faith in and loyalty to Jesus Christ as Eternal God and Himself the source of enabling Spirit, under whose impulse we can never rest until God's Name is hallowed, His Kingdom is come, and His Will is done, in earth as it is in heaven.

These, then, are the great marks of the Christian revelation. It is given in objective events for

[1]Philippians iii. 14.

minds divinely illumined to interpret, so that it covers by implication the whole range of experience both in its subjective and in its objective aspects; and the decisive event in which it culminates is a historical Person who manifests a selfless love and claims in answer a loving obedience, not to precepts suited only to one age, but to a Spirit by which men may live in every time and place—for it is the Spirit of selfless love.

What then is the authority of this revelation and how does that authority become effective? If revelation took the form of formulated truths it would presumably be a duty to believe those truths; but it must be recognized that this would not of necessity be a converting influence; 'the devils also believe and tremble'. But to revelation taking the form of a Person the response must take the form of personal loyalty. The revelation is not primarily in propositions concerning Christ to which my intellect may assent; it is in Christ Himself, to Whom my whole personality must bow. This includes, of course, the homage of the intellect, which must accordingly seek to apprehend according to its own mode of activity both Christ Himself and our relation to Him; this is the work of Christian theology; it issues in the great Christian doctrines. These are of profound importance, because they point men to the actual revelation; but they are not themselves the vehicle or the content of that revelation; they are the exposition of it, as the textbook of Astronomy is the exposition of the starry heavens. The revelation is the fact—Jesus Christ Himself.

The appeal exercised by this revelation is to the whole Personality; the authority exercised is over the whole Personality. Therefore response to it cannot be reluctant; only where it is willing does it exist at all. This is the answer to Shelley's complaint: 'If God has spoken, why is the universe not convinced?' It is because the revelation is given in a Person to persons. Thus it becomes a principle of judgment, as the Fourth Gospel insists. 'This is the judgement, that the light is come into the world, and men loved the darkness rather than the light.'[1] Christ moves about among men; some believe and some reject; and therein they are judged. All saw the outward acts; only some 'beheld His glory'.

Thus revelation exercises its authority by calling forth responsive obedience and love from those who are able to receive it. Because it is given in a Person to persons, it acts through, not either apart from or against, the free motion of their wills. There is a compulsion upon the soul, but it is exercised through freedom; God puts forth His power upon us, but our servitude is our perfect freedom.

[1] St. John iii. 19.

In face of such revelation the intellect is completely unfettered. It may criticize the records through which it apprehends the revealing fact; indeed it must; it shows its own loyalty in so doing. There is no suppression of any human instinct or capacity in the response we make. The authority of revelation is spiritual; not, therefore, coercive in the sense of constraining conduct against heart or will; not intellectual in the sense of constraining judgment by irresistible evidence; but spiritual—that is to say, personal—wherein all faculties are responsive according to their appropriate activities.

The first response is personal surrender to the majesty disclosed—'we beheld his glory'. But this is not enough. Revelation must make good its claim to that surrender not only by the impression which its first impact makes, but by its capacity to render experience as a whole even more intelligible and by its power, when accepted, to guide men through the perplexities of life. Yet in this life our ability to apply this criterion is limited. We may demand that it should offer the starting point for a fuller and richer philosophy than we can frame without it; we may claim that on the arena of history taken broadly it should in some measure exhibit its saving power. So much in principle is right. But it always may be our lot to live at a time when the data for combining the revelation with other factors are lacking, so that only with some further advance of knowledge shall we be able to exhibit the philosophical unity to which we none the less believe that the revelation affords the focus; and History as known to us is, and always will be, so contingent a fragment, that we may be unable to trace the saving power of the revelation even though it be there at work; for indeed the revelation itself would lead us to believe that only eternity truly resolves the riddles of time, and we shall not expect to do this perfectly in our present life.

While therefore the criterion is sound—the criterion of philosophical completeness and practical effectiveness—yet our capacity to apply it is not great; and in the end our responsive homage is offered to Him whom we believe to be God manifested in the flesh, not because we have applied the criterion, but because, with ever clearer vision as we obey and adore, we behold His glory: it is personal homage to a Person, the testimony of the Holy Spirit from within us to the objectively uttered Word of God.

By the Rev. Father SERGIUS BULGAKOFF

*Translated by the Rev. Oliver F. Clarke
and Miss Xenia Braikevitch*

I. WHAT IS REVELATION?

Revelation takes for granted the existence of
something which is being disclosed, or of a mystery which manifests itself to us. Mystery does not
consist merely in that which is unknown or secret,
which may or may not be imparted, manifested or
withheld. Nor can the knowledge of it, when perceived, be exhaustive or in any way adequate. Mystery remains *above* human understanding, and can
never be exhausted by reason. Logically exact
thought can never penetrate mystery, which is
above human and worldly comprehension. Yet at
the same time it is a necessary characteristic of
mystery to disclose itself, indeed were it not for
this fact it would not be a mystery. In revelation
it is the *transcendent* which discloses itself, though
it is not exhausted by such disclosure. The nature
of mystery is such that it is equally possible for it
to exist *above* revelation, as well as disclose itself
through it. Mystery ceases to be a mystery, if it

is not disclosed, or, on the other hand, if it is resolved and exhausted by the process of revelation. It is equally characteristic for a mystery to disclose itself and to remain hidden, for it always remains a mystery in the process of being disclosed. In this sense it is God, for God according to the patristic definition is equally a relative concept. God is God for the creature, He is a God who is revealing Himself. Revelation, therefore, is of the very nature of Deity.[1] God is a self-disclosing Mystery.

Mystery undergoes modification in this very act of self-disclosure; it is the object of revelation, though to the same extent its subject also. An understanding of mystery is not by any means the concern of the seeker alone, that is of the recipient of revelation, because for him mystery is transcendent and unattainable. Revelation is the impact of the One who reveals Himself on the one who receives revelation. Revelation is the personal act of a personal Deity. 'I am the Lord thy God,' says

---

[1]Thus in the depths of the Absolute we distinguish two antinomically correlated (though mutually unreferred and reciprocally incongruous) definitions of the Absolute which is God; darkness, and the unapproachable light of the Absolute, and of His revelation as God the Creator in creation. A further investigation of this basic contrast lies beyond the limits of this article, for which see *The Light that Never Sets*, 1917; *The Lamb of God*, 1934; *Essays on the Trinity;* and other writings by the present author. (None of these at present exist in English: Translators.)

Jahveh. 'I am that I am.' Revelation is a *personal* act, which takes place 'face to face'.

The Subject of revelation, as the One who discloses Himself, is correlative to the subject who receives revelation. In this sense revelation is a *dialogue*, a colloquy between God and His creation, angels and men. While the fullness of revelation belongs especially to man (Cp. I Peter i. 12; Ephesians iii. 9-11) revelation represents a *divine-human* communion, an act of God *within* man, and the consequent acceptance of God by man. Revelation implies an encounter and a conversation, God's covenant with man. Man is a personal being, and revelation proceeds from the *Person* of God to the *person* of man. It was so in the case of Moses on Mount Sinai, as well as in the case of Isaiah, Jeremiah, and all the major as well as the minor prophets. It was so in the case of the apostles and other men who were moved by the Spirit of God 'at sundry times and in divers manners' (Heb. i. 1).

Every human personality, however, is a part of the whole of mankind. Each personality is its representative, is man in the all-inclusive sense. Although God's revelation is actually received by one particular person, and cannot even be expressed in words as an experience, as far as its content goes it is intended for the whole of mankind, if not in fact, at least in principle. Moses on Sinai 'went up unto God, and the Lord called unto him

out of the mountain, saying, Thus shalt thou say
to the house of Jacob, and tell the children of Israel' (Exodus xix. 3). A prophet who receives
revelation is always a mediator. Consequently,
revelation does not become disintegrated into a
series of separate, personal, episodic acts, but is
accumulated and integrated in the destiny of mankind. In this sense it is both an action and a fact,
a 'deposit' of faith, a revelation which is going on
all the time. Regarded in this way it is life eternal
for the creature. The creature, which knows only
'in part', can never exhaust the ocean of Deity. It
is true that we have the promise that in the age to
come we shall know God no longer in part and in
a mirror darkly, but face to face, even as also we
have been known; not as children, but as men
(I Cor. xiii.). This, however, is a distinction of
degree only, and does not destroy the qualitative
difference between the Creator and the creature:
the creature can never aspire to know God as He
knows Himself, God will never cease to be for man
a mystery in the process of revelation. Revelation
will never stop, because it is *life eternal*. 'And this
is life eternal, that they should know thee the only
true God, and Jesus Christ, whom Thou hast
sent' (John xvii. 3).

Christ revealed and manifested God to man in a
new way. He is the door through which we enter
into divine knowledge, as we learn to know God in

Him through the Holy Spirit. Nevertheless this is
not a case of attaining to a rationally complete
knowledge within time, it is rather an eternal process of acquiring understanding. The eternal life
of the creature is nurtured by the divine and actually becomes identified with it, but the distinction
between God and His creature, between the One
who discloses Himself and the one who receives
revelation remains indubitable and eternal. The
deified man, who is a god by grace, partakes of the
divine life, but remains a being different in nature.
Revelation represents a divine-human communion.
The revelation of mystery in itself is a secret
between God and man. One must be capable of
receiving revelation and worthy of it. A stone, or
even an animal, is incapable of receiving revelation. Nor can even man bear revelation in greater
measure than it is given him, for 'man shall not see
me and live' (Exodus xxxiii. 20; Cp. Judges xiii.
22). Revelation represents a divine impact on
man, but this act is never a forcing of his nature
(as in the case of *deus ex machina*). It presupposes
a certain reciprocity, or *a likeness between the image
of God and man*, in fact, their correlatedness. It is
necessary for God to be in a certain sense human
and for man to have something divine within him,
if man is to become a recipient of revelation, and if
intercourse between God and man is to become
possible. The Bible expresses this relationship be-

tween God and man by saying that man was
created after the image of God, and consequently
that God contains within Himself the Primordial
Image of man. Thus there is set up, as it were, a
'ladder' between God and man, which can be used
for ascent and descent.

We can most easily grasp this by considering
the Incarnation and Pentecost, which both represented the descent of God from on high. According to the Chalcedonian dogma the two 'natures'
—the divine and the human—are united in Christ
in the life of one Person, so that Christ is perfect
God and perfect man. God is finally disclosed in
the God-man, while man accepts God's revelation.
We have another analogy in the descent of the
Holy Spirit at Pentecost, when the gift of the Holy
Spirit, 'grace', overshadowed and inspired human
nature, thus uniting itself with it. At the same time
—and this is the most important point—man preserves all the fullness of his humanity, without
being dissolved or consumed by the divine fire
which descends from heaven. Revelation is divine
humanity *in actu*, a living identification of the divine with the human, in spite of the undoubted
difference between them.

We should learn to interpret the 'image of God'
not as a sort of 'quality' or 'resemblance'—for
what question can there be of resemblance?—but
realistically, as a similitude in difference, and a

difference in identity. God's image in man is a
reality, a real power, its true humanity. It cannot
be destroyed by sin, or even by original sin, and
because of this it is the foundation of the Incarnation. It is that by means of which man was capable
of meeting and accepting into himself the Logos
when It was incarnate, and the Holy Spirit when
He descended from heaven. God's image is the
spark of Deity in man, God's Spirit, which God
breathed out of Himself when He created man.

Various attempts were made in patristic literature to describe more precisely God's image in
man: some identified it with reason, others with
free will, and all of them limited it merely to the
spiritual nature of man, disregarding the body as
something foreign to the image of God. The body
was consequently degraded to the position of a
species of 'accident', and even to that of something
unworthy of man, contrary to the clear meaning
of the Bible narrative of man's creation, and in
particular the creation of the body (Genesis ii. 7).
It is futile error to *limit* God's image in man to
some *one* part of him, for it belongs to the man as
a whole, in so far as his integrality has not been
changed or, more accurately, corrupted by sin.
Man is a creaturely god both in the spirit and in
the body, in their mutual relatedness, and also in
his personal being as well as in his nature.[1]

[1]See the theological addendum at the end of this contribution.

II. NATURAL REVELATION

There exists a natural revelation of God in His
creation, in nature and in the human spirit. All
men are created 'of one blood' for the purpose of
seeking 'the Lord', who is 'not far from every one
of us' for 'we are also his offspring' (Acts xvii.
24-28, the speech of St. Paul before the Areo-
pagus. Cp. his and Barnabas' speech at Lystra,
Acts xiv. 17). Divine revelation goes on in nature
(*vide* Psalm xix. 1 ff: 'The heavens declare the
glory of God: and the firmament sheweth His
handywork. One day telleth another: and one night
certifieth another. . . . Their sound is gone out
into all lands: and their words into the ends of the
world.'). Rom. i. 19-20 refers to the same thing:
'Because that which may be known of God is manifest in them [the Gentiles]; for God hath shewed it
unto them. For the invisible things of him since the
creation of the world are clearly seen, being perceived through the things that are made, even
his eternal power and Godhead.' The moral law
in man and his conscience also testify of God: 'In
that they shew the work of the law written in their
hearts, their conscience bearing witness therewith,
and their thoughts one with another accusing or
else excusing them' (Rom. ii. 15). These words
give adequate recognition to the principle of natu-

ral revelation, and therefore to natural religion—
to 'paganism' as such, which, nevertheless, was
called into Christ's Church and showed itself
worthy of the call in so far as it accepted Christ,
Who had been rejected by the synagogue. It is
necessary to reflect upon the fact that such natural
revelation in man was possible and to consider its
limits.[1]

Natural revelation is based on the very same
fact of the presence of God's image in man, who
already contains within himself the divine essence,
because of the very manner of his creation. But, it
may be said, would this not lead to an admission
that Deity is immanent in man, or that man himself is immanent in Deity? And might we not tend
—as a result of recognizing the divine basis in
man—to drift into the twilight of pantheism with
its confusion or identification of God with the
world? We see examples of such merging in pan-
theistic philosophies in Spinoza (*Deus sive natura*),
in German idealism (Schelling and Hegel), and in
Brahmanism. But the teaching on the image of
God in man can only be developed when we recognize the *personal* God, the Divine Trinity, Which
is supermundane and transcendent in Its hypo-

[1]The existence of natural revelation is fully admitted both by
the Catholic and Orthodox Churches (see particularly Scheeben:
Handbuch der katholischen Dogmatik. B. I. Erstes Buch, Erster
Teil). The position is much more complicated in Protestantism.

static life. The world has its basis in Deity, but as it was created 'from nothing' it can never be identical with Deity. (This philosophy should therefore be described not as pantheism but as 'panentheism'—$\pi\hat{a}\nu$ $\dot{\epsilon}\nu$ $\theta\epsilon\hat{\omega}$.)

Man, according to the plan of his creation, is not only the centre of all creation, uniting in himself all its many threads, but also one who has been endowed with divine depths. He is a god by grace. In natural revelation man is revealed to himself in all his divine depth and he is in himself inspired by this depth—as man by his humanity. At the same time by the very discovery of this divine foundation in himself, he demands the descent from above of divine revelation for which he waits with ardent longing. Yet already in himself and in creation man recognizes the 'marks of Deity' and receives a natural revelation concerning it. Man has within himself the first principles of eternity, which is immersed in time and reflected in the face of time. Therefore man is subject to development within time, to genesis. The depths of his own being are a mystery even to himself, which is gradually unfolded in the process of his life. This self-revelation of man is founded on the divine life, which becomes disclosed in him. Actually our self-consciousness is incapable of embracing the depth of the human spirit in its entirety. Natural revelation is responsible for the fact that man's know-

ledge of himself comes to include that divine revelation, which has been enshrined in him through
the image of God. Man discovers the seal of Deity
both in his own spirit and in nature.

But the clarity of this self-revelation is obscured
by original sin which distorted the whole of man's
being, though it never succeeded in destroying its
divine foundation, namely, God's image. A catastrophe has taken place in the process of human
self-revelation. It has displaced the centre of
human nature, and man has lost that initial state of
harmony in which he was able to comprehend both
himself and the world. Man's realization of himself resembles a distorting mirror, which reflects
the images of existence in an equally crooked and
partial manner. Natural revelation, which is at the
same time human self-revelation, is still man's
possession as St. Paul himself testifies, though it
is subject to error and illusion. Deliberate deceit
and error can also permeate it as a result of sin.
The content of natural revelation or 'paganism' is
determined precisely by complicating factors of
this nature, which cannot be eliminated by man's
own efforts. Pagan religions should not by any
means be regarded as devoid of any positive religious content. Precisely the reverse is the case. We
must admit that every one of them contains a kernel of divine revelation. Man recognizes this revelation within himself, he discovers within the

depths of his own being this image of God within himself. But this revelation of self can only be realized by a sinful man through a medium which is itself sinful. The kernel of truth is imbedded in a mass of falsehood, human sensuality, and passion (all sorts of 'psychologisms' in fact) and there are all manner of evil 'enchantments' which make for further complexity. In the face of pure truth the revelations of paganism (as containing a mixture of truth and falsehood, with a frequent preponderance of the latter) become quite intolerable, while any close contact with paganism involves a form of spiritual infidelity. 'What concord', asks St. Paul, 'hath Christ with Belial?' (II Cor. vi. 15). Hence we can understand the irreconcilable attitude adopted towards paganism by the Old Testament prophets and by St. Paul in the New Testament, as well as by some of the apologists such as Tatian. Nevertheless this attitude is combined with a more positive recognition of the existence of certain truths in paganism, 'of the Christianity prior to Christ,' to which we get references in Clement of Alexandria and St. Justin Martyr. Only in the light of Christianity can we rightly discern and impartially appraise the positive elements in natural religions, which are manifested in the dialectic process of their history. In the light of Christianity alone can paganism be interpreted, not as an error and an abomination, but also as a 'natural' Old

Testament for Christianity—that it was so is borne out by the fact that pagans accepted the 'good news' of Christianity.

Further, it is not only the dialectics of the religious process in heathenism which are characterized by such natural revelation, but also the dialectics of philosophical thought. For pagan philosophy, undoubtedly, is not merely a meaningless form of religious speculation, but also a positive seeking after God. In its own realm philosophy cannot be compared with a purely religious experience, but there is no doubt that it follows its own methods of seeking after God and knowing Him. This is sufficiently confirmed by the contributions made by Greek philosophy to Christian theology. Natural reason is also akin to the divine *Logos*, for it also contains religious revelation, even though such revelation may be vitiated by purely human elements. The same would be true of art, which, as a vision of Beauty, is naturally connected with the Holy Spirit. This is also evidenced by the contribution made by paganism (more especially by Egyptian and ancient art) to Christian worship. And in general it may be said that Beauty, wherever it shines forth in the world, always witnesses to God.

Thus we should fully accept the human, natural revelation which man discovers within himself and within the world in the image of God.

III. DIVINE REVELATION

Man in his capacity of a creaturely, cosmic being possesses his own peculiar revelation of God's image. But God created man within the context of a particular, given world, and bestowed on him an independent existence, yet not in order that man should remain shut up within himself in a state of self-satisfaction or be separated from God in his own self-sufficiency. Such a mode of life is satanic; it is the way of the prince of this world. Man is called to union with God. God desires to be *all in all* both for the world and for man; God wants to reveal Himself to man, and to deify him. God's image in man is a living bridge between heaven and earth, a vessel for divine revelation. God's love of man—by the power of which creatures exist—is expressed in God's communion with man, in revelation, while man's love of God, enshrined in man through the image of God, finds expression in his search for this revelation. Man, who is destined to be a creaturely god by grace, partakes of the knowledge of God and holds communion with Him through revelation, and becomes a god-man in this divine-human intercourse. While growing in the knowledge of God, he learns how to know himself in the depths of his spirit, and there is a real contact between the image and the Prototype.

What is it then that comprises the revelation of God in man in the simplest meaning of the word? God *speaks* to man, and man partakes of divine *life*. The God-inspired word and its mysterious power—such are the two ways of divine revelation in man. Revelation, above all else, represents a dialogue between God and man. God speaks to man in his own human language, and man listens to God's word and interrogates Him, using the human reason. The word of God is at once human (audible to man), and divine-human. The divine *Logos* is also the human *logos*, just as the Name Jesus is the proper name of the God-man. This identity in difference is the fundamental fact and prerequisite of revelation. Furthermore man remains himself, and without losing his humanity is allowed to experience God's touch, to partake of divine life, *pati Deum*, to experience the mystery of a living communion with the Deity. All this takes place in a manner identical with that in which is was possible for the divine and human in the life of our Lord to become One, and for the Spirit of God, in descending on the Apostles and other men, to abide in them uniting Himself with their human spirit, and through it with their divine-human spirit too. *Humanum capax divini*.

The voice of the supernatural in the natural as such could never result in revelation. Such a voice would simply be inaudible, and entirely alien to

man, it could never reach man or affect him.
Revelation must necessarily be a union of the
divine with the human. This living divine-human
entity constitutes the image of God in man, it implies the existence of the primordial image of man
in God. God discloses Himself to man in the Word
as the Truth, and in the Holy Spirit as Life in
Their dyadic inseparability. The Nicene-Con-
stantinopolitan Creed says of the Holy Spirit:
'Who spake by the prophets.' The Spirit is not the
Word. But here the word of the Word is inspired,
it is 'spoken' through the prophets by the Holy
Spirit. And such, generally, is the 'di-unity' of
divine revelation: it is the Word as a certain content, and at the same time as an inspiration of life,
'at sundry times and in divers manners' (Heb. i. 1).

'Natural revelation', as we have seen, is the self-
revelation of man in his divine foundation. In contrast to this revelation, in the exact sense of the
word, is the *action* of God in man. This is a descent of
God. It is an act of God's will, a fulfilment of love
which God evinces for man. It is a real meeting
between God and man, such as is pictured for us
in numerous events in the life of mankind both in
the Old and the New Testaments. Moreover, it is
to be noted that the full humanity of man is preserved in such intercourse. Man is even more fully
established in the process, he wrestles with God
for his humanity, as Israel struggled all night with

the Mysterious Stranger, to use the symbolic image employed in the Old Testament: 'and there wrestled a man with him until the breaking of the day. And when he saw that he prevailed not against him . . . he said: Let me go, for the day breaketh' (Gen. xxxii. 24-26). And Jacob-Israel said: 'I have seen God face to face, and my life is preserved' (30). But man is called not only to wrestle with God, but also to be His friend ('And the Lord spake unto Moses face to face, as a man speaketh unto his friend', Exod. xxxiii. 11).

God discloses Himself, according to His will, but revelation is fulfilled through man. Therefore it concerns his humanity. This quality of humanity has its own destiny, the principal moment of which is the upheaval which occurred in man at the Fall. Prior to this man was capable of direct communion with God, he could 'converse' with God, and the paths of revelation lay open before him (this is expressed in the stupendous mythological images of Gen. i.-iii. 'And they heard the voice of the Lord God walking in the garden in the cool of the day', iii. 8). But after the Fall the image of God in man was obscured, man began to resist revelation and hid from God, thus all the human side of the divine-human process of revelation becomes burdensome and difficult. The divine rays only pierce this darkness of man's natural existence through certain elect souls and because of certain providential actions of God in various events of human existence. Revelation is only possible because of the election of a definite and very inconsiderable portion of mankind to a particular destiny. This enclosed vineyard of the Lord becomes the place where God reveals Himself on earth.

It is equally important to remember in this instance both the difficulty of this whole process —in which God Himself takes on Himself the labour of conveying His revelation to the rebel man—and the actual possibility and effectiveness of this revelation. Original sin was not an insuperable barrier between God and man. God's image in man shone forth, even though it was in a measure obscured. Man in the Old Testament remains susceptible to revelation, and God's efforts to disclose Himself to man 'at sundry times and in divers manners' (Heb. i. 1) met with growing success. A true knowledge of God was gradually firmly implanted and, as it deepened, began to shine forth in the Chosen People, who had been entrusted with the treasure of God's Word. In addition to this, and of no less vital importance, is the fact that this knowledge of God became fulfilled in life as a certain holy reality. The genealogy of Christ our Saviour is a corroboration of this fact and the crowning point of the process is the appearance on earth of the Virgin Mary, the Mother of God. In her, man becomes completely

responsive to revelation, and the whole creation
speaks through her lips: 'Behold, the handmaid of
the Lord; be it unto me according to thy word'
(Lk. i. 38). It now became *possible* for the Incarnation to take place. This possibility had been ever
present in God, but it had to become so in man as
well. God's revelation was accomplished in a
complete union of God and man, in God's 'descent from heaven' to His creatures. This revelation was primarily fulfilled in the Incarnation of
the Word. The first verse of the Epistle to the
Hebrews—which has already been quoted several
times—interprets it precisely in this way: 'God,
who at sundry times and in divers manners spake
in time past unto the fathers by the prophets,
hath in these last days spoken unto us by his Son.'
Jesus by Himself and in Himself revealed God,
the Heavenly Father. Our Lord was a personal
revelation of God concerning God, of the Son
concerning the Father. He actualized this divine
revelation in His divine-human life, which manifests a union of two natures, two wills, two energies,
and equally of two words: the divine Word and the
human word, the *Logos* and the *logos*. But God's
revelation to man was not completed by the Incarnation alone, for it was followed by Pentecost, the
descent of the Holy Spirit from on high. Pentecost
was an inspiring of human life by the divine, so that
the fullness of the divine-human could be realized.

This revelation, which though in a sense final was still capable of extension, took place in the New Testament Church, in the Body of Christ, which is moved by the Holy Spirit. Revelation continues in the Church for it is the Church: 'the fellowship of the mystery, which from the beginning of the world hath been hid in God . . . to the intent that now unto the principalities and powers in heavenly places might be known by the Church the manifold wisdom of God (πολυποίκιλος σοφία τοῦ Θεοῦ), according to the eternal purpose which He purposed in Christ Jesus our Lord' (Eph. iii. 9-11).

IV. REVELATION AS HOLY TRADITION

Revelation is not bestowed on an individual in his isolation, but on man in the all-inclusive sense, and thus on the whole of mankind through him. Though in its particular form of expression revelation is delimited by time and space, nevertheless it retains its significance for the whole of humanity through its living tradition. It is a case to which we may well apply Christ's words that there is nothing secret which shall not become manifest. For every single instance of revelation is enshrined in the 'sacred history' of mankind, is preserved in its 'holy tradition'. We must begin by grasping the fact that revelation is not only 'the letter', but the life which is sealed by it, a real intercourse between God and man which takes place 'at sundry times and in divers manners'. The primary factor is life; the letter and tradition are of secondary importance.

Revelation constitutes the history of mankind in the portrayal of its relationships to the Deity, and in this sense it is the history of its surrender to the Deity which is handed on from generation to generation. Revelation comprises not only a memory of the past, but also the present living and abiding tradition. Whilst moving within time, past and present are an integrated whole, so that it is always maintained in the fullness of life. If we cast a mental glance over the history of mankind to the present day, we cannot help observing that the whole content of this history is comprised not merely in its original chapters, but is rather enshrined in the whole of its life. Tradition primarily represents a certain sacred reality. In Genesis we have the history of the world, of its creation by God, but the whole of this history is somehow included in our life. The 'historical books' of the Old Testament narrate the history of the Old Testament revelation as associated with the destinies of the Chosen People. But the whole of this history is recapitulated in the genealogy of Christ our Saviour. This applies not only to His written genealogy but also to His living humanity. The humanity of our Lord is the living tradition of the whole of mankind from the creation of the world to our time, focussed in the life of the Chosen People. Tradition as a living revelation is the realization of divine-humanity which is still going on, a communing of man with God, man's deification.

Moreover revelation as tradition consists not only in the knowledge of God, or a true faith, but equally in life in God, God's gift of grace. For the man of the Old Testament this life of grace was determined by the Law and sacred ceremonial, by the institution of sacrifices and the worship in the Temple, by the ministrations of the kings and prophets, in a word, by the whole fullness of Old Testament life, of the circumcision of the flesh. The New Testament tradition of mankind consists in a fullness of life in Christ through the Holy Spirit, in a unity of faith and sacraments, of the gifts of grace, in a unity of Church love—in all the abundance of the revelation granted to us. In other words, revelation represents the divine-human life of the Church and our own participation in it. It is just as impossible to set bounds to this life or to exhaust it, as it is to determine the inner limits of the Church. Revelation is life in God, a process of deification which is in progress—god-manhood.

On these grounds we should never attempt to contrast or separate, or, even worse, mutually to exclude Holy Scripture and Holy Tradition, as two different forms of revelation. The whole of

this doctrinal controversy between Catholicism
and Orthodoxy on the one side, and Protestantism
on the other, is based on a misunderstanding. For
to make such a comparison is in itself a misunderstanding. Tradition, as the life of the Church, does
not represent *one* of the sources of revelation or of
the methods of its preservation, but revelation
itself *in actu*, life in God through life in the Church.
Tradition is the Church, as the living unity and
integrality of present, past and future, as god-
manhood. All its possible manifestations are included in this life of revelation: there are, besides
the sacraments, grace and the prophetic spirit
which abides in the Church, Holy Scripture and
other books, which are literary and material evidence expressing both the revealed life of the
Church and its thought. Revelation is the Church
itself, mankind as the Church, god-manhood in the
process of becoming.

We can speak in a twofold manner about revelation: as an act—a sacrament of communion with
God, which is taking place—and as something
which has already been accomplished and sealed
by certain external signs, inscribed on the tables of
stone of human history. Revelation is the activity
of the Spirit of God, who descended at Pentecost;
it is equally life in Christ, who abides with us now,
and ever, and unto the ages of ages. The external
facts of revelation can only come to life and receive

power through this actual ever present revelation, according to the words of the Apostle: 'the letter killeth, but the spirit giveth life.' 'It is the spirit that quickeneth; the flesh profiteth nothing: the words that I speak unto you, they are spirit, and they are life' (John vi. 63). This is the distinction, according to our Lord, between the word as a fact of the 'flesh', and as an act of spirit. Such an approach does away with any interpretation of revelation which would confine it to any one, special, external fact (expression)—for instance to the content of Holy Writ. If the last were true it would result in a reversion to Old Testament legalism, as demonstrated by the 'scribes and Pharisees' and so frequently denounced by our Saviour. The Word of God, if we pause to consider the precise meaning of the term 'word', is not a book or a document, but Holy Writ, which only exists *in* the Church and *for* the Church, which only lives and becomes real in the life of the Church. Outside the Church the Bible is an ordinary book which dies in dead hands, and becomes a mere object for smart criticism. Actually the Bible is revelation for a life of revelation, viz. for life within the Church. In unaccountable and unfathomable ways God's revelation, through the medium of the Word of God, touches individual hearts. This clearly manifests the *efficacitas* of revelation. But this method of influence is neither

magical, nor is it a case of purely human revelation. It is the breath of the Spirit of God, an extended revelation, a contact between man and God.
It would be true to say of the process that the
Word of God is always written *in a new way* in
men's hearts. The story in Acts viii. about the
eunuch of the Queen of Ethiopia gives us further
light on the above. He was reading the 53rd
chapter of Isaiah—the book which might be described as the Old Testament Evangel—whilst
travelling. Philip asks the eunuch: 'Under-
standest thou what thou readest?' He says: 'How
can I [understand], except some man should guide
me?' (30-31). Thereupon Philip 'began at the
same scripture' and gave him the good news of
Jesus. Philip baptized him after he confessed his
faith in Jesus Christ as the Son of God, and the
Holy Spirit descended on him (35-39). This shows
us the complexity of the whole process of revelation. In this particular case it originates as the
result of reading a particular book. It is not, however, limited to this fact, but demands an act,
needs special inspiration, which is first conferred
through the speech of the Apostle, and later by the
Holy Spirit Himself. It is the same process as that
described in Luke xxiv. 45, where we read that
Jesus 'opened their mind, that they might understand the scriptures'. Revelation is an individual-
catholic act, through which the isolated individual

is included in the corporate life of the Church. Revelation does not begin with one separate man and end with him. Every man possesses it for himself, but not alone, or in isolation. The immanent criterion of revelation is, therefore, the life of the Church. The Church witnesses from within and also outwardly to the truth of revelation—such is its postulate. An opposite conclusion follows from this; namely, that the entire life of the Church— whatever its expression—constitutes a continually extended revelation. In consequence of this alone, revelation can never be limited to one source— even if this one is the most important source, namely, the written Word of God.

Because revelation is concrete it can never admit an equal significance in all its external records. These records differ one from another, in themselves, in their character, in their relative importance, in their content and in their significance. In addition life includes its own shades and distinctions, even when these cannot be expressed in an absolute theological formula. It is a fact that even the sacred books of Holy Scripture are not all of equal importance. We distinguish between the Old and the New Testaments. In the Old Testament we make a distinction between the prophetic and the historical books—for instance, between the book of Isaiah and that of Esther. In the New Testament we distinguish between the Gospels

and the Epistles, and even among the latter we
make a difference, say, between the First and the
Third Epistles of St. John. This would apply to an
even greater extent to other records of revelation in
the life of the Church, which have been preserved
by tradition. For example, the texts of the Holy
Liturgy are not of the same value as those of other
Divine Offices which are of less importance. The
Creeds and the other theological definitions of the
Oecumenical Councils are not equal to the writings
of the most authoritative of the holy Fathers. The
entire revelation, nevertheless, constitutes a closely
knit and concrete unity. In particular instances,
any one of its records may acquire a greater or
lesser significance under the influence of the
Spirit of God and the individual characteristics or
the peculiar receptiveness of special persons. The
context of the sacred canon corresponds to this. It
does not in the least degree represent a legal code,
a system of theology, or a catechism. It resembles
rather a large collection of mountains and hillocks,
a fanciful conglomeration, the component parts of
which would appear quite haphazard in their
structure. It is a crystallization of history in all the
whimsical fancy of its ornamentation.

We know that this sacred canon does not by any
means include all the writings of God-inspired
men (cf. the Epistle to the Laodiceans, and other
Epistles ascribed to St. Paul, λόγια Χριστοῦ, etc.).

On the other hand, we find that it contains books whose worth was contested at various times. The Bible is a divinely inspired monument of the history of revelation. In a similar way various later records of the tradition of the Church represent, as it were, a diary of Church history, which bears on the life of revelation. It would be true to say in this sense that revelation—in its relation to the quickening and revealing Spirit of God—is both the Incarnation and the descent of the Holy Spirit in the process of their realization. The Spirit of God which moved on the face of the waters in the state of original chaos, continues to abide in creation, uniting with man's spiritual essence, while all the multiform paths and records of revelation serve partly as occasions and means, partly as special acts of revelation. Through them and in them revelation is continued.

V. HOLY SCRIPTURE

The Protestant world venerates Holy Scripture as the unique source of revelation—as the 'Word of God'. In the Orthodox and Catholic world Holy Scripture is included in the general context of the tradition of the Church, which actually established the canon of sacred books. The tradition of the Church is looked upon as the principal source of revelation, as the word of God, inspired by the Holy Spirit, who 'spake through the prophets'.[1]

In what sense is Holy Scripture the Word of God, and how should we interpret its 'inspiration'?[2] I assume that no one can any longer, in our time, advocate the theory of a mechanical inspiration of sacred books. This theory either regards the writers as passive instruments in God's hands, or interprets the process of writing as dictation from the Holy Spirit. 'Inspiration' is not a question of *deus ex machina*. It is not an act of God which coerces man, and to which he is subjected apart from his own will—it is a divine-human process. The usual term 'Word of God' should be interpreted in a wider sense than that conveyed by its literal meaning, for it would be better described as the divine-human word. 'Inspiration' comprises human inspiration, which by special divine con-

---

[1] The usual formula of the Orthodox-Catholic catechism which states that the revelation of the Church consists of Holy Scripture *and* Holy Tradition, thus putting them side by side as two distinct sources, is obviously unsatisfactory. Firstly, there are not two such sources but one: the Tradition of the Church, which includes Holy Scripture. Secondly, in the general context of Church Tradition the Word of God undoubtedly occupies a position of primary importance, as it checks all the rest of Church Tradition.

[2] This question has a long history and there is an extensive literature on the subject. Compare the parallels in the following articles—'Inspiration' in the *Dict. de theol. Dogm. Cath.*, vol. vii. 2, and in *Real Encycl. der prot. Kirche*. Bd. ix.

descension is illuminated by the Spirit of God, so that it can come to include divine inspiration also. 'Inspiration' in general is only one particular form of revelation, which, as has been pointed out above, represents a meeting between man and God. At such a time man is not passive. On the contrary, he is pre-eminently active: he experiences the highest tension in his humanity, as well as in his individuality and personal genius.

In order to understand still further the nature of the Word of God we must accept the full implications of the position that God's word is equally the human word. God speaks to man in human language, and human words are used to express the Word of God. Man in this process is not in any way deprived of his humanity, but becomes, so to speak, human in a much deeper sense. Holy Scripture is the revelation of God Incarnate, of the God-man, the Son of God who is also the Son of Man; of the Word of God, and the human word. This is equally true of the Scriptures prior to the incarnation of the Second Person, at the time of the Incarnation (in the very preaching of the Word, and during His sojourn on earth), and after the Incarnation. Similarly the Holy Spirit 'spake by the prophets' before Pentecost, at Pentecost, and after it, through the lips of the Apostles and other men of God. In this particular sense there is no actual distinction between the

Bible and other monuments of tradition which have originated in the life of the Church according to the principle contained in the words 'it seemed good to the Holy Spirit and to us'. Holy Scripture is written by men. It has been filled with divine power and has thus become a medium of revelation, the Word of God. It should not to the least degree be treated as an oracle, as is frequently the case when it is interpreted as the transcendent Word of God. The 'friend of God', Moses, listened to the Word of God in the darkness and fire of Mount Sinai, but this Word was inscribed by him on the tables of stone and entered in the Book of the Law when he came down from the mountain. An exaggerated and one-sided bibliolatry treats the Word of God as a transcendent oracle. Such interpretation reminds us of the origin of bibliolatry, when a legalism of the letter of the Bible—a definite reaction in the direction of the Old Testament—replaced, to a certain extent at least, that of the Church of Rome. If, however, we accept the Word of God as a divine-human word, we at once dispense with any question as to the *limits* of its divine inspiredness in relation to every single letter and punctuation mark. In so far as it is the human word, the *whole* of it is written by man, if one may put it this way, with a human pen and by a human hand. While in so far as it is, at the same time, the repository of the Word of God and is inspired by the Holy Spirit, we must learn to discern it through the medium of the human word.

We should therefore regard the Holy Scriptures, because of their worth and sacredness, with especial care and reverence. But the same considerations compel us to strive to comprehend more fully the concrete historical form of the Scriptures, so that we can understand them not only in their divine content, but also in their human guise. One cannot turn the relative into an absolute, and identify eternity with the concrete and the historical. The particular form we possess is at once the vessel which contains and the curtain which hides the Word. It is that through which the Word shines though it is not actually identical with this word in itself. In this aspect the Word of God represents a spiritual miracle, which is incessantly repeated. It is the miracle of the supra-humanity of the human word, of its permeability in relation to the Holy Spirit. In this sense Holy Scripture represents a particular expression of divine-humanity, which originates in the Incarnation of Christ and the divine inspiration of the Holy Spirit. A miracle does not consist in the annihilation of human nature by divine omnipotence, so that the human word is actually changed into the very Word of God. It involves a process in which the human word is made transparent to the Word of God. It is an example of the union of the Word of God and the word of man, which is 'without separation and without confusion'. It is 'without confusion' in so far as the human word maintains its distinctness and its own nature in the Holy Scriptures, in spite of the fact that the scriptures contain the Word of God. It is 'inseparable' because the Word of God is also the human word, and does not permit the use of any other form of expression for itself. We have here a particular case of the application of the Chalcedonian dogma which treats of the unity of two natures in Christ—the divine and the human—which are 'inseparable and without confusion'. Holy Scripture is another special means by which the manifestation of God's image in man takes place in its relation to the Primordial Image. The image corresponds to the Primordial Image, for it contains it within itself, though it does not merge with it and differs from it.

Important practical and exegetic postulates result from such an interpretation of the manner of revelation in the Word of God. We can only accept the Word of God as such—as it is contained in the Scriptures—when it becomes an object of special revelation within revelation. The principle of the general *efficacitas* of the Word of God, which makes it comprehensible to every person who reads it, is insufficient in this case. Here we have a special activity of the Spirit of God, who enlarges the mind 'for an understanding of the

Scriptures'. It is the work of personal inspiration which takes place not in a state of secluded individualism, but in one of catholic consciousness or *sobornost*.[1] In other words, Holy Scripture can be the Word of God only within the Church and for the Church.

Further, only the Church has proved competent, through the special inspiration of the Holy Spirit, to *witness* to the Word of God in Holy Writ, viz. to establish the canon. The canon constitutes a revelation about revelation. The Church similarly comments on the divine content of Holy Scripture. This does away with all pretentious individualism, according to which every individual who possesses a Bible finds himself capable of and called to define the mind of the Church. Such an attitude does not in any way minimize the truth that whenever revelation is received—in this particular instance through the reading of the Word of God—the process represents a personal act in the life of the given individual. But at the same time it is an act of the Church and Catholic, for the Church as a whole is inspired by the same Holy Spirit. This inner unity of the Spirit finds

[1]In Russian the adjective *soborny*, corresponding to the noun *sobornost*, translates the word 'Catholic' as applied to the Church in the Creed. As *sobornost* and *soborny* have a wealth of meaning not found in any equivalent English words, we have used them wherever the symphonic character of Catholic consciousness seems to be indicated. (Translator.)

further expression in external unity, in an individual checking of each case with the mind of the Church. Such is the necessary postulate of belonging to the Church. This examination in every special case is carried out differently, in accordance with the particular requirements.

It is this fact which serves to explain the erroneousness of the thought, which is sometimes expressed by representatives of biblical legalism, namely, that the Bible is the foundation of the Church, and not the reverse. But this idea that the Bible, as the Word of God, is given only to the Church which witnesses to the revelation therein, can also be applied in quite a different sense. All that is human lies within the context of history and is therefore subject to variation. The sacred books also, in their human aspect, are subject to the influence of history. They belong to a definite epoch, people, or culture and are stamped by the individuality of their authors. Historical relativity is one of the characteristic marks of this human aspect. This historical form belongs entirely to the realm of biblical science. When the study becomes more exhaustive and more concrete we can read these human writings better and render them more exactly. Critical science should never of course exceed the limits of its natural competence, which it constantly did and continues to do by turning historical relativism into religious relativism.

Nevertheless its true religious worth lies in the fact that it does not allow the relative to be turned into an absolute. Every historical epoch reads the Bible in its own way, which corresponds to the general level of its thought and knowledge. It is impossible for us to return to the historical artlessness, and the state of blissful ignorance, characteristic of the ancient Church in its attitude to the sacred text. Such an attempt, even if made, is foredoomed to become a prey to hypocrisy and deceit, and could never be realized. The fact, however, that our historical orientation is changed has no decisive religious significance for our perception of the Bible as the Word of God. We know very well that all our modern conclusions about biblical texts (however relative and insecure, they do provide us with guidance at present!) do not in any way represent the last word of science or the only conceivable attitude to the biblical text. They form a part of the historical life of the Bible within the Church. They only destroy the incorrect assumption that one can regard the human embodiment of the Bible (or rather its present actual form) as a sacred oracle. In this sense, therefore, the Bible belongs to history and moves within it as we do. Such a conception does not in any way make the *religious* content of the Word of God relative. The reverse would be true. The true purpose of scientific investigation is the destruction of barriers which hinder us in our understanding of the Word of God. These barriers arise as a result of the obvious lack of coordination between the historical image of the Bible and the consciousness of modern man, and lead to *religious* misunderstandings. Science sharpens our powers of perception and enables us to distinguish the Word of God in the context of the word of man.

If we admit the existence of a certain historical relativism in the human element in the Word of God, we arrive at one more conclusion, namely, the possibility of drawing distinctions in the relative importance of the different books of the Bible. This arises from interpreting revelation in a concrete manner, instead of applying a category of canonical sanctions in the abstract. We assume, of course, that all the books included in the canon possess a certain divine content and form a part of Holy Scripture, to which the Church bears witness. But the fact that they are included in the canon and are consequently formally equal, is not sufficient for their full evaluation. In spite of their official equality, as it were, we cannot admit with any degree of sincerity that the book of Esther, for instance, is equal to the Psalter, because it is included in the canon; or that the book of Judges is equal to the Gospels; or that the entire Old Testament is equal to the New Testament. This does not minimize the importance and necessity of all

these books once the Church has deemed fit to
include them in the canon, but their value is only
evident in the full context of the Bible, which is a
complicated and multiform unity. But in our attitude to these books in practice there is room for us
to choose the more vital for ourselves. The truth of
this is externally confirmed by the uncertainties
evinced at the time of the canonization of these
various books, while in our time it is silently confirmed by the difference made in using the books
in practice.

The concreteness of this revelation, which we
draw from the Bible, is generally expressed by the
fact that its divine content does not constitute
something static, something that has been given
once for all and is now petrified. We receive it
equally in history and through history according
to our personal and historical development and
age. The Word of God is stamped with the seal of
eternity, it is therefore sufficient for all ages, and
yet it goes on revealing itself to us; which is the
reason why it has not been disclosed completely as
yet. As we turn the pages of history, so the pages
of the Word of God are turned over before us. This
is quite obvious from its history: for mankind in
the Old Testament revelation was confined to the
Old Testament; New Testament mankind has the
New Testament. This, however, does not imply
that the full content of the latter has been revealed

to us. This is particularly true of its most mysterious and essential parts: the prophecies, apocalypses, and the eschatological sections, which are written with the intention of revealing that which is 'to come'.

VI. THE AUTHORITY OF THE CHURCH

Revelation is not given to man in seclusion or isolation, but in Catholicity; though it is accomplished in persons and through persons, it is given to the whole of mankind in its history. Within time crystals of revelation are formed, its golden particles and precipitates sink to the bottom, and that which is described in technical language as the deposit of faith is thus found. This amassing and storing of revelation already commences in the depths of the Old Testament, from the early days of the history of mankind. Written revelation in the form of sacred books begins to emerge. They are added stone by stone to the building of the sacred canon. This canon preserves the living tradition of the faith and of the covenant, the law, and divine worship. A new epoch emerges in the New Testament revelation, when revelation is enriched both through life and through the written word. The New Testament books are included in the canon of the Bible. The life of the Church, its worship, dogma and canons, as a living tradition, are enshrined in definite objectivized forms of revelation. The statics of revelation find expression alongside of its dynamics. Yet how do they come to be defined? What are the conditions for preserving a given revelation as a deposit of faith?

Here we move from the life of the spirit, which represents a supra-empirical realm, to the domain of historical experience, where the Church exists not only as the 'invisible' Church, as the supra-historical Body of Christ, but also as a visible human institution, possessing an external organization, as well as definite organs of expression. But can *organs* of revelation exist and is such a thing possible? We must draw a distinction here between the organs which safeguard revelation which has already been given, and the acceptance of and witness to revelation which is taking place and will take place, in the past, the present and the future. We must make it quite plain that there never has been and never can be an external, unchangeable, and permanent organ of revelation in the shape of something established by the Church. The Spirit bloweth where it listeth, and no one can imprison it in external forms. The prophets and the apostles are not appointed by law, but are a manifestation of the life of grace. In the same way the Oecumenical Councils do not represent a canonical institution for the reception of revelation, as is frequently supposed, but are themselves a fact of revelation. We must never forget that revelation, as interpreted above, is always a *miracle*, and a miracle can never be established by, or be subject to law. The fact that Moses ascended Mount Sinai for the purpose of receiving revelation did not mean that he had special authority to pronounce *ex cathedra*, but represented a direct command and providence of God. The same is true also of prophets who were chosen before their birth (Jer. i. 5).

Now disregarding for the moment all the individual examples of revelation, let us focus our attention upon the general fact of revelation in the life of the Church. We find that the Church safeguards the truth and bears witness to it and we must admit that the possession of this truth by the Church is in itself a perpetual miracle, affirmed by the common faith of the Church which is 'the pillar and ground of the truth' (I Tim. iii. 15). In what manner and on what occasions does the Church construe truth, detaching it from falsehood and error (for *Deus ecclesiae suae non deest in necessariis*)? It is not merely that it is impossible to answer this question ; it is not merely that there can be, but that there should be, no answer. The Church is the Body of Christ, which is inspired by the Holy Spirit. It represents a mystical unity (*sobornost*) and to this unity the truth is disclosed. It is absurd therefore to imagine that an oracle exists which dictates the truth of revelation to the Church. Such a notion is contradicted alike by the nature of the Church and that of revelation itself. If such an oracle were to exist it would stand above the Church and outside it. This is our main theological difficulty in accepting the Vatican dogma of the Pope as infallible *ex sese, non ex consensu ecclesiae*, in so far as his prerogative bears on the present and the future, and is not confined to the past.[1]

Protestantism is one-sided, because in its reaction to Papacy, in the name of freedom in the Church, it insists on a complete absence of any

[1]We should distinguish here between two possible manifestations of the authority of the Head of the Universal Church. The first expresses, as it were, a pre-eminence of position as the representative of the Church. In this sense the Pope would be the mouthpiece of the Universal Church. This idea agrees with the general trend of tradition in the Church in relation to the primacy of the Roman see. It is quite compatible with the conception of the *sobornost* of the Church, which becomes hierarchically organized from top to bottom. The second interpretation, which represents the ultramontane principle, triumphed at the Vatican Council (although even now it is possible that it may receive a more acceptable interpretation in the future). According to its definition—*ex sese, sine consensu ecclesiae*—it seems to involve the abandonment of the idea of *sobornost*, which is replaced by institutional prophecy *ex cathedra*, thus introducing a dogmatic oracle. Catholic theology, however, at its best, does not wish to abandon the principle of *sobornost*, and attempts to combine it with the Vatican dogma even though the arguments used appear unconvincing. A moving example of such an attempt may be seen in Scheeben, *l.c.* 80-96.

external organization in the Church, in relation to the life of revelation. In practice, however, this negation is not realized. Protestantism also recognizes revealed truths which are powerfully and authoritatively safeguarded by the organized Church, which possesses its corresponding organs. Does not the Bible itself, in the context of its sacred canon, represent such a fact of revelation? It originated in a miraculous and supranatural way, it is revelation, which has at the present time become a *law* of faith. It is safeguarded by the Church, and that, not only by the 'invisible' or mystical Church, but also by the institutionally organized Church through the corresponding organs of authority. It is not only the sacred canon which has thus been preserved by the Church in its tradition. The basic dogmas of faith (in spite of their having been watered down by liberalism and minimized by criticism) also find adequate protection and have authoritative witness borne to them in the Protestant hierarchy. It is also true to say that this hierarchy, whatever its organization may be, also acts in *soborny* concord with the whole of its community. Moreover, any anarchy excused by the idea of general prophetism, is utopian. Such anarchy is an illusion, which is untrue to reality and contradicts the nature of the Church. Even Quakerism, which aspires towards unmediated revelation and denies the possibility of any deposit of faith as well as authoritative organization, retains the Bible. This means in practice that it admits the Bible as a fact of revelation and consequently as a deposit of faith, at least in the context of the sacred canon. It also recognizes the fact of the existence of a community, which possesses a definite dogmatic basis and certain principles of organization. For an unorganized society simply cannot exist, it always becomes transformed into a 'herd'. Consequently the Church must always be an organization of faith, that is, of revelation.

The Church, therefore, in its empirical and historical being is not merely an organism, but also an organization. It goes without saying that such an organization is hierarchical. It cannot be an institution where the hierarchy is appointed by purely human methods of election. Such an institution, moreover, represents an objective gift of grace and in this sense also a deposit of faith. It is that which has been purely conditionally and inexactly described as the 'apostolic succession'. The hierarchy of the apostolic succession originated and exists primarily as a sacramental organization, which is based on the power bestowed for the celebration of the Eucharist and of the other sacraments. But this power is of such unique importance that as a result of its possession the hierarchy becomes generally the centre of authority in the

Church, and in particular receives special authority
to teach. It is therefore natural for it to serve as a
sort of mouthpiece of the Church which proclaims its truth. Then it is similarly the guardian
of all the truths which have found expression
within the Church and have been accepted by it.
It is obvious, of course, that the hierarchy does
this as an organ of the entire body—viz. of the
Church. Even in this, its most unquestionable
prerogative, the hierarchy is not divorced from the
Church. It is not *ex sese, sine consensu ecclesiae* for
it acts in harmony and unanimity with the whole
Church. *Charisma infallibilitatis*, which is revelation, is bestowed on the entire Church inspired by
the Holy Spirit. The Church, however, in its empirical and historical existence, constitutes an
organism of grace, a Catholic body, which is not
amorphous but organized.

The prerogative of the authority of the hierarchy to serve as the mouthpiece of the Church
and the guardian of revelation applies, however,
only to the content of the revelation which has
already been given. The hierarchy can never become an infallible organ of revelation, interpreted
as its oracle, because this would be contrary to the
very essence of revelation, which recognizes no
forms or limits, and which is equally within reach
of the priest Ezekiel and of Amos the herdman of
Tekoa. Prophecy is always expressed in this very

way. In relation to newly proclaimed truths of revelation the hierarchy, though it continues to act as the mouthpiece of the Church, can only pronounce on them in so far as it can really grasp the truth within the Church, which has the right of accepting or rejecting the decisions which the hierarchy has made on this subject. In such a case the hierarchy only possesses conditional infallibility *donec corrigetur*.[1] Were the hierarchy (and here the one Pope, or a 'collective Pope' comes to the same thing) to possess such infallible authority, it would involve the repudiation of the gift of prophecy, which is bestowed on all within the Church; it would in practice do away with revelation as a divine-human process. To put it more precisely, the hierarchy alone would then represent the whole body of the Church. Such a conception would obviously contradict both the idea of the Church itself, and that of revelation as such. Everything within the Church is both individual and Catholic. It is natural, of course, that when Catholic theology develops its teaching on the infallibility of the Pope it usually regards him as the Vicar of Christ Himself, that is one who in practice occupies our Lord's place. This means that in so far as Christ is the New Adam, who

[1]See the chapter on 'The Hierarchy'—on the external authority of the Church, in my book *The Orthodox Church* (The Centenary Press).

contains within Himself the whole of mankind, so far the Pope as such[1] also represents the New Adam, as representative of the whole of mankind within the Church. But it is difficult to reconcile such an interpretation with the idea of the body of the Church, which consists of various members in their multi-unity.

VII. REVELATION AS A CONTINUOUS PROCESS

Has revelation come to an end, and can it ever cease? If our tendency is to interpret revelation statically, not as life but as a deposit (as something given), and not as action but as an accomplished fact, we shall answer this question in the affirmative. The 'last times' commence after the Incarnation and Pentecost, for God's revelation to men had been accomplished in principle through the deification of creatures by the Incarnation. This accomplishment, nevertheless, is not merely an event in time and a fulfilment in our own era. It holds good for eternity as well, and the entire life

[1] The Catholic doctrine actually wavers in this case between two irreconcilable and mutually exclusive points of view: according to the one, St. Peter, as it were, lives and acts in the Pope; according to the other the Pope is the Vicar of our Lord Himself. These doctrines originated at different times and from different sources, but they have been artificially combined.

of mankind is determined by its further manifestations in this aeon and after it. Revelation comprises both the life of the separate individual within the context of his whole destiny, and the life of the whole Church and mankind. It is a life of an ever growing knowledge of God. On the one hand this includes the personal acceptance of revelation. On the other hand, the Word of God, this book of life, the 'eternal Gospel', is continually being read afresh, and in the process is always being seen in a new light with a deeper penetration into its significance. In a similar way the truths proclaimed by the Church in the form of dogmatic definitions, for example, the dogma of the Holy Trinity or of the Incarnation, become an object of personal revelation ('And we will come unto him, and make our abode with him', John xiv. 23). A man who becomes a dwelling place of the Holy Trinity, through the power of the Holy Spirit, receives a living revelation of that which is enshrined and included in the phrase 'deposit of faith', which so often has a scholastic ring about it. Man receives a similar living revelation of God in the sacraments which give man an experience of communion with God in accordance with his general spiritual condition. Revelation does not consist only in a conveying of knowledge through the word, but in the communication of that life which cannot find expression in words.

The problem of 'dogmatic development' or the possibility of new dogmas, is very closely connected with the above. Usually one is forced to give both a negative and a positive answer to this question. The negative answer is given in the sense that within the Church, which represents life in Christ under the guidance of the Holy Spirit, the fullness of truth already exists, in relation to which there can be nothing new. But we find that the positive answer is in a sense equally true. The fullness of truth is further disclosed in history through new manifestations of itself, or through new dogmatic definitions. This is amply confirmed by the history of dogma. The plenitude of truth is not a treasure which is kept locked up, it is abundance which always flows into life and enriches it. It follows, therefore, that dogmatic development can never cease in history. It is, further, subject to varying tempo and dependent on the characteristics of a particular epoch.

At the same time we should never lose sight of the fact that apart from the constantly occurring process of dogmatic definition, history itself is a process of a continually expanding revelation of life. New problems emerge in history and new revelation is given. In order to understand this truth more fully in connexion with the whole process of revelation in history, we must again reject any interpretation of revelation as an external, mechanical process, and learn to regard it as a divine-human interaction, a 'synergism'.

History is essentially 'apocalypse'—the revelation of God through the thunder of events. For each man his own life is such an apocalypse, and likewise every historical epoch conceals its own revelation. History calls us to a *prophetic* understanding, and we must answer its call by prophetic insight and daring. There is an unwritten, unauthorized revelation which is even now rising up within our own souls, though it must pass through a certain trial before it can be recognized by the Church. The main questionings of our own epoch concern matters of practical Christianity and of creative Christian effort in the domains of social and cultural life. The whole social question is like a sphinx regarding us with dead eyes and saying: Unriddle me or I shall devour you. Human society, as it exists at present, is no mere aggregate of atomic individuals but a social body which leads an animal life of its own and is torn by interior conflict. But it must become the body of Christ and so be identified with the Church. The Church itself must assume responsibility for social life— thus manifesting her prophetic office in the social sphere. This new revelation is now being born into the world amid spiritual travailing pains which promise to be creative and fruitful.

There is, however, a still wider and more vital

problem with which our era is confronted. We have to face the growing *secularization* of life, the recrudescence of paganism in its coarsest and most non-religious form. Even the heathenism of primitive peoples seems to be pious in comparison with the state of spiritual desolation in which contemporary humanity finds itself. But the Church cannot reconcile itself with such a secularized culture. She cannot thus surrender her power to the prince of this world. The whole of life must belong to her, and be inspired and sanctified by her influence.

This cannot come to pass unless the Church become conscious that she is being called to creative effort. She must overcome her tendency to ascetic or eschatological indifferentism (we may even call it nihilism) which results in the inward separation of the Church from the world. Otherwise pagan humanism will never be vanquished by a Christian humanism. Yet our time cries out for a Christian humanism—a new revelation regarding the *world* and the place of human creative effort in it. New problems are thus put before the Church. Of course imaginary questions may be asked to which no answer is possible, but to all true questions regarding our life there applies the promise: Seek, and ye shall find. We look now for a new revelation of the Church's power in this world's life. Without such revelation and such achievement the fullness of the time is not yet accomplished, and the end of the present aeon cannot be reached. The end of history, or of this age, will be marked not only by a catastrophic interruption but also by this fullness.

The Second Coming of Christ, the 'parousia', will constitute the revelation which will complete our aeon. The other event will be a new vision of the power of Pentecost which will complete the 'transfiguration' of the world, when there will be a 'new heaven and a new earth'. All these are monumental symbols of the epochs of revelation— in history and beyond history, in this age and the next, in eternity.

Revelation, as a life in God, means life eternal, eternity itself, and eternity has two facets in relation to ourselves. First, the temporal, in which eternity appears in the form of infinite duration (which may be good or evil according to the content with which we fill it); second, eternity in a *qualitative* sense, as an unfathomable depth of life which is being revealed, that is, 'life eternal' as an ever progressing knowledge of God (John xvii. 2-3). The creature can never attain to an adequate or exhaustive knowledge of God, who therefore reveals Himself eternally to it. The deification of man, when God shall be all in all, does not contradict this, because when the Kingdom of God finds expression in creation in this way, the creature's life in God will be expressed in the form of revelation from a boundless ocean of divine eternity. This is, actually, a continuous divine-human process, an actual unity of the divine and creaturely Sophia, an eternal dialogue between the Transcendent and the immanent, between God and His creature. The image gazes upon the Primordial Image and becomes radiant in Its light. The Sun of the Primordial Image communicates Its light to Its image. The Incarnation is not only an event which took place once for all, but an act which goes on perpetually; Pentecost too is not only a single happening, but incessant divine inspiration. The hidden life of the Holy Trinity is communicated to creation.

ADDENDUM

The theological term I use to express the resemblance of man to God is that of *Sophia* (Σοφία). Man is created in the image of the *divine* Sophia, and in this capacity he is himself determined as the *creaturely* Sophia. Sophia in God is the principle of His self-revelation in divine life. God's idea, the divine world, exists above and prior to creation. God, who abides in Trinity, is the Father, who is disclosed in the Word by the Holy Spirit. The unity of nature (μία φύσις) and the unity of life in Him are revealed in Him as a certain absolute, eternal *content*, as Truth, which achieves reality in Beauty. This content is the divine Word of the Word, of the Second Hypostasis, which contains *all* within itself (John i. 2), and this ideal *all*, the organism of ideas, is brought to reality and life by the life-giving Spirit.

Sophia exists for the tri-hypostatic God. It belongs to His Hypostases in their separateness (corresponding thus to the inner qualities of *each One* of Them), as well as in Their *Unity*. It cannot exist outside and apart from the Hypostases, and yet, in spite of this, it is not a Hypostasis. It cannot be identified with any single *One* of the Hypostases (for example, the Hypostasis of the Word), nor with the Holy Trinity in its entirety, though it cannot be separated from them. Dogmatically and metaphysically we distinguish in God the Hypostasis (or the Hypostases) and nature ($\dot{v}\pi\acute{o}\sigma\tau a\sigma\iota s$ or $\dot{v}\pi\sigma\sigma\tau\acute{a}\sigma\epsilon\iota s$ and $\phi\acute{v}\sigma\iota s$), but at the same time we also affirm their inseparability. This $\phi\acute{v}\sigma\iota s$ is the depth, the root, of Deity. Sophia is similarly $\phi\acute{v}\sigma\iota s$, but as the content of self-revelation represents the life of Deity in Itself. In the Holy Trinity the Father is the Beginning, the Hypostasis which reveals Himself, while the Son and the Holy Spirit are the Hypostases which reveal the Father. This revelation is the Divine Word, in Whom the Holy Spirit abides pre-eternally, *the ideal manifested in reality*, the divine Sophia[1] which is, consequently, determined by the dyad—the Son and the Holy Spirit, who both reveal the Father.

Sophia is actually the divine nature ($\phi\acute{v}\sigma\iota s$), which was re-united in the God-man Christ with the creaturely-human nature according to the Chalcedonian dogma. Such a union *de facto* testifies to the likeness in image between the two natures, the divine and the human, or—which is the same thing—between the divine and the creaturely Sophia, for they are compatible in the same life of the one Hypostasis of the Logos. The complete congruity and correlatedness of the two natures, which *can* be so united in the God-man, is thus fully confirmed. Another way of

[1] I have explained the bases of sophiology in its connection with triadology in a number of my works, in particular in the treatise *On Divine-humanity*, vol. i; *The Lamb of God*, 1934, vol. ii; *The Comforter*, 1936. Cp. with my articles: *Chapters on the Trinity*, *The Hypostasis and Hypostasity*. (All these works are in Russian only.)

putting this is as follows: the divine Sophia as the revelation of divine nature represents the pre-eternal, divine Humanity, which corresponds to the Primordial Image of creaturely humanity. Both these natures are disclosed as the one *Divine-humanity* or Sophia, both in divine and creaturely being. In the writings of St. Basil the Great, St. John of Damascus, St. Maximus the Confessor, and some of the other Fathers[1] we come across the general idea that the world was created on the basis of divine $\pi\alpha\rho\alpha\delta\epsilon\acute{\iota}\gamma$-$\mu\alpha\tau\alpha$ which are obviously akin to Plato's ideas. The divine seeds of being are plunged into non-being, into a world of *becoming* (Plato's $\gamma\acute{\epsilon}\nu\epsilon\sigma\iota\varsigma$), and give rise to the being of the world as its entelechy (in the Aristotelean sense) purpose and reason, foundation, and ultimate aim. Man, as the subject of humanity in its multiple hypostasis, is the creaturely Sophia. Divine-humanity is the hidden foundation of man's creaturely humanity. Man is an emergent God-man. This possibility which was given to man in Christ finds its complete fulfilment in Pentecost, though it also took place in the Old Adam through the power of the Holy Spirit.

Moreover, this link between man and God in Sophia, which forms the basis of human being or of divine-humanity, makes man at once capable of, and called to accept, divine revelation, makes him in a word the subject of revelation. *Humanum capax divini.* Man becomes capable of religion in the sense of a true communion with God. The fact of religion expresses the divine-human in man. It is in practice that unity of God and the creature which is of the nature of revelation. *Revelation is a divine-human process,* and cannot be conceived of outside divine-humanity. Any break in this divine-human link, however small, would reduce revelation to a mechanically coercive action of God *on* man, an example of the *deus ex machina* principle. It would, in fact, involve a contradiction. The principle of revelation finds expression in the following words of Christ. Referring

[1] See the passage from the Fathers on the creaturely Sophia in my book on Our Lady, *The Burning Bush*. Paris, 1926.

to Psalm lxxxii. 6, 'Ye are gods: and ye are all the children of the most Highest,' He adds: 'He called them gods, unto whom the word of God came.' We may note also our Lord's words about His friends: 'No longer do I call you servants; for the servant knoweth not what his lord doeth: but I have called you friends; for all things that I heard from my Father I have made known unto you' (John xv. 14-15). Only God's friends can 'hear', viz., comprehend revelation, which is the ladder between heaven and earth, a vital merging of the divine and the creaturely Sophia. God can only reveal Himself and speak to beings who are like Him, and who bear His image, that is to men and to angels.

V

By the Rev. M. C. D'ARCY, S.J.

———

Like so many other words of theology, revelation can be used in a strict, and in a general or loose sense. Long controversies, which usually end in the clearing up of an initial confusion, have produced the strict definition. If, therefore, we keep to the strict sense, revelation must be carefully divided off from other theological meanings such as inspiration, infallibility, faith and our natural means of knowing about God. I do not think, however, that it is the intention of the editors of this book to confine its subject matter to the strict meaning, and indeed the other contributors have ranged over other subjects. I propose, therefore, to begin with the strict meaning and having exhausted that to pass on to something more general. By so doing it will be possible, I hope, to check certain confusions often made, and at the same time to comply with the intentions of this book.

It is part of the essential faith of the Catholic

Church to distinguish between two orders, the one natural, the other supernatural, and in accordance with this distinction the Vatican Council contrasted 'truths which have come down to us from heaven' with the 'interpretation of religious facts which the human mind has acquired by its own strenuous efforts'. The former are truths of revelation, truths, that is, which have been made known to man by God through channels which are beyond the ordinary course of human nature. These include the truths which God 'at sundry times and in divers manners spoke in times past to the fathers by the prophets', and above all what God 'hath in these days spoken to us by his Son, whom he hath appointed heir of all things, by whom also he hath made the world'. The Epistle to the Hebrews goes on to emphasize the unique importance of this revelation by saying: 'therefore ought we more diligently to observe the things which we have heard, lest perhaps we should let them slip. For if the word, spoken by angels, became steadfast, and every transgression and disobedience received a just recompense of reward: how shall we escape if we neglect so great salvation, which having begun to be declared by the Lord, was confirmed unto us by them that heard him?'

The attitude of the early Church towards this revelation is made clear by these words, and is confirmed by St. Paul's strong assertion: 'though we, or an angel out of heaven, preach a gospel to you besides that which we have preached to you, let him be anathema. . . . For neither did I receive it of man, nor did I learn it; but by the revelation of Jesus Christ.' What then is directly communicated by God Himself and is called by the Apostle Paul the gospel of Jesus Christ is revelation in the strict sense of the word. The early Church regarded it as a deposit of faith, and throughout the ages the Church has regarded itself as the guardian and interpreter of this divine communication and communion with man, and it has cast out from itself whosoever attempted to adulterate this divine message, 'for we are not as many, adulterating the word of God, but with sincerity, but as from God, before God in Christ we speak'.

Now a number of questions arise in connexion with this explanation of revelation, such as the extent and character of it, the adequacy of human language to render it faithfully in every age and tongue, the meaning of development, and the conditions required on the part of the recipient both to understand it and to accept it. Such questions directly or indirectly bear upon it, but it is confusing if we mix up with this particular problem the quite different one of inspiration and infallibility, or assume that the knowledge given to us of God through the works of nature or the moral order or natural beauty or, if there be such a thing, by the religious sense, can be called revelation or any equal title. Certainly this has not been the historical tradition of Christianity, which has always separated sharply the gospel revealed to us in and by Jesus Christ from all else, be it philosophy or natural religion. It is customary to use the word for private communications which have been made to mystics and saints, but always with a caution. The Church is prepared to examine these private revelations and even to make use of them, but it resolutely refuses to put them in the same category with the deposit of faith, and indeed tests them by their agreement or disagreement with what has been once for all given by Christ, the Son of God.

Such then is the strict meaning of revelation, and if exactness were rigidly demanded, to this we should keep. As it is, no matter what more general meaning from now on is to be employed, the proper sense should always be borne in mind —and for this reason. If the world wishes to know what are the credentials and character of Christianity, it ought to be told what is its consistent teaching throughout its history. The Church is too old and far too deeply committed to spring a surprise in the year 1937, and so the bright ideas which appear in books, telling us at long last what

Christ meant and what the authentic message of Christianity is, may, perhaps, have an intrinsic value, but they ought to be called by the name of their authors instead of by the name of a faith which has abided man's questioning two thousand years. If we cannot know by now what the revelation of Christ is, then we must dismiss Christianity despite all its comfort and arguments as a failure, and reluctantly deny the claims of Christ. At the beginning of this century this obvious criticism was not felt, to judge by the liberty indulged in by authors when writing on revelation; and at the time the main streams of Reformation theology seemed to be differing more and more among themselves and from orthodox Catholicism. A change, however, has taken place, and it is remarkable how much writers on this subject are now willing to admit as common ground. There is, for instance, general agreement about the transcendence of God and the consequent supreme authority inherent in whatever communication He may make to man. Furthermore, this revelation is to be found in a unique manner in the teaching of Christ, and therefore the proper attitude of man is first to be attentive and obedient to it and only secondarily to weigh it and perhaps judge it in terms of immediate experience. The Eastern Orthodox Church has, moreover, retained its firm belief in the mystery of God's holiness and the elevation of man by grace into a supernatural order of union with God through Christ, and now once more an austere tradition of Protestantism is prominent in what is known as the Barthian theology. The Catholic rejoices when he finds so many speaking with one voice and saying in striking tones what he holds with all his heart and soul.

The fact, however, that the preceding essays have covered much of the ground does not make my task any the easier. It is tempting to concentrate on points of difference and ignore what would make only for repetition. On the other hand to introduce a note of controversy is neither gracious nor suitable, and so I propose to explain those points of the Catholic doctrine, which have not been sufficiently developed or else have been denied, owing, as I hope, to a misunderstanding of their meaning. Almost all, as I have said, are agreed on the authoritative character of the Christian revelation within a Church. The variance of interpretation begins after this in the delineation of the *rôles* held by the Church and the individual and the relations of authority to freedom and reason. In the present reaction against the liberal and individualistic interpretation of the Christian faith the necessity of a Church is emphasized. Nevertheless it is often difficult to make out what function the Church has and how it is composed. To leave it vague is surely a mistake because vagueness hands us over again to sheer individualism. If I do not know where the general will is to be found I must decide by my own will and I shall be tempted to make up a general will to suit my own desires and beliefs, and claim sanction for it. To escape from this predicament some fall back upon the text that the Holy Spirit will lead us into all truth, and see within their own denomination or, if they are generous, amid the jostling differences and contradictions of the multitudinous sects of Christianity some unity of truth and even of authority.

The real battle, however, begins when the claims of divine revelation and individual judgment have to be reconciled. It is now seen that the former must have sovereign power to direct the world into the ideal contemplated by God. On the other hand the place of experience and scientific method are to many equally important, for in the discovery of these, they think, consists the glory of modern development, *i.e.* the superiority of modern culture over the past. Both these claims can be so put as to be in fact irreconcilable, and Christianity has suffered much from extremists. If it be said that revelation is like a stone dropped from heaven, then all that successive generations of man can do is to stand around and admire; if on the other hand all is left to the mercy of human opinion and interpretation, then in time the original will be so written over and glossed as to be uncertain if not unintelligible. There can be no doubt that in the early centuries the word of God, given in and through Christ, was regarded as sacrosanct; and the occupation of the early Church, as 'the pillar and ground of truth', was to carry on that one live word into the darkness of paganism. To the early Protestants the sacred word carried the same august and uncontaminated majesty, and it was not until the scientific mind penetrated into all forms of belief that a change in attitude took place. That that change ran to excess will now be freely admitted, but in checking it and condemning it we must not forget the reason for its success. Those who contrast the attitude of faith with that of reason are generally guilty of superficial generalization, as are also those who define the current opposition to Christian belief as rationalism. It is not rationalism, if by that word we mean the old belief in reason. The modern does not believe in reason; he is frightened of the *a priori*; he does not live by faith but by hope. He eschews the certainties of his forefathers and prefers that expectation which comes from experimentation and is confirmed for the while in part by sensible experience. We are, of course, no less dogmatic now than in former times, but our dogmatism is one of impatience and prejudice and not of contemplative assurance. The scientist prefaces all his theories

188

with an 'if' and regards his ultimate premisses and principles as assumptions, and he has taken to heart more than he knows the philosophic conclusions of Kant. Reason, therefore, to the modern means a disbelief in deductive reasoning and a hope that by the means now in use the progress and improvements so much in evidence may be maintained.

It is this attitude of mind of which we must take notice and not any particular argument. Indeed argument and reason in the old sense are conspicuous by their absence. The religious thinker of today has no use for the reasoned proofs of the existence of God and the old apologetics for Christianity. He suspects them because he has adopted, often without knowing it, the mentality of the empirical scientist, and with the encouragement of the same scientist he invents a new defence for his religious beliefs, which belongs to a genre that the scientist can appreciate. This defence is by what is called religious experience. I have in another place[1] tried to assess the value of this new defence of religion and I believe that it must pass into an old argument in new guise before it can be said to have efficacy. But what now it is relevant to notice is that experience is an alternative to reason, and it is surely odd that the very persons who condemn the faith for

[1] See *The Nature of Belief*.

failing to be reasonable should try to correct this failing by recourse to what is of its nature alien to reason.

The explanation of this is possibly as follows. It is currently believed that in the old and orthodox tradition revelation was treated as beyond reason or, like a stone, incapable of progress, and that its upholders believed in some oracular form of explanation and transmission. Such a view was felt to be outmoded and to believe in it could only harm the interests of religion. Religious thought of this kind was bound to be ostracized, whereas the great need of the day was to cut away the dead branches of religious dogma and give new sap to the trunk. Now, the scientific methods of the day offered the only rational methods of advance, and they gave full scope for personal and private judgment. Hence there arose a school, which for convenience can be called liberal. This treated the Christian religion in exactly the same way as any other historical or scientific inquiry. But, as to many the effects were mainly subversive, a hint was taken from Kant and contemporary philosophies, and religion and science were separated. Just as morals and aesthetics were judged to have a value in experience which could not be estimated on so-called rational or mathematical methods, so too religion was given a new lease of life by right of a unique experience which it contained.

The changes which have taken place in national and international politics have been reflected in religious movements, and while the old liberalism and modernism survive they have to be reconciled with a surging tendency to absolutism. No longer does the so-called theory of immanence occupy the mind exclusively. The problem now is to harmonize it with the transcendence of God—and the emphasis lies rather on the latter truth. The individual, too, however sacred his rights, must hearken to the wisdom of a Church, and sects which once warred together bitterly, now seek terms for an alliance and are prepared to consult even the Catholic Church because of its long history and tradition of philosophic and theological thought. In this period of transition it is possible also to discuss points without bitterness and, indeed, to recognize the points worth discussing. In every sphere of thought, philosophical as well as religious, there have been times when extreme and crazy fashions have so captured the fancy that there has been much ado about nothing and serious-minded thinkers have had to possess their souls in patience. But in times of crisis the real problems force themselves to the front, and it would appear that we are now living in such an age. This simplifies our task; and I propose to take some of these questions, which will fit under the wider definition of revelation, and to give the Catholic solution to them in the course of an explanation of the Catholic belief.

These questions concern first the bearing of the Christian revelation on man and its relevance to man as he is now, secondly both the character of that revelation as rational or supernatural and the way, rational or supernatural, by which it can be accepted by the individual, and thirdly the medium by which it is communicated; whether that be by private experience or by a Church and if by a Church, whether the Church should speak oracularly or rely essentially on the growth of knowledge by science and history. These questions cover the main topics, but there is a preliminary one, which if it be not cleared away will cause confusion. This can be put as follows: If man be in touch with a living being, to be called God, will not that God be constantly revealing Himself through physical nature, the souls of men and their activities, and in morals and art? The simple answer to this is, Yes, but in a way which is distinct from that of revelation as understood by Christianity. This reply must, however, be amplified, and it can best be done by some comments on the nature of man. Experience and knowledge teach us that he cannot be fashioned by exterior force like a stone or piece of wood. He cannot grow without exterior help but he must meet it half-way and cooperate. As a being gifted with intelligence and conscious desire the means of self-perfection lie partly at least within himself, and if this be so he must understand what he wants before adopting it. This law is admittedly modified in human societies because it is just that the most experienced and the wisest should be believed before their regulations are fully understood. Wisely therefore adults as well as children follow the orders of doctors and lawyers and electrical experts and navigators and statesmen. But while they obey they reserve to themselves the right to disobey and the teaching they accept falls in principle within the compass of their own individual judgment. It remains true, therefore, as an ideal that in matters of human knowledge understanding should precede the act of the will. Any plan, then, that would impose from without a perfect life which can only be sought and gained from within must seem foolish, and so we need not trouble ourselves to inquire whether God has chosen to do this.

It is quite a different question, however, whether God has cooperated in order to help man to be wise and good and live in peace with his neighbour. If life were a paradise, we might expect that God would work in and through the very powers of man which He created, and in that sense man would be left alone. I say 'in that sense' because, God being closer than hands and feet and nature being His work and image, the loneliness of man would be only apparent. In fact, we know that this world is anything but a paradise, that millions have little more than a buried intelligence, that passions take charge of even the best minds, and that men and women will scarcely confess their spiritual being, much less comprehend it. We live in a disordered world where wrong is claimed as right and the weak go to the wall despite all legislation and the simple are deluded by the sophistries of the clever. If we choose to call the discoveries of man in an earthly paradise by the name of revelation, there is more reason for calling what God has done in this labouring world by the same name. For His way, as it would appear, is still to proceed through natural means to a knowledge of Himself —but through man's own stress and needs. Man comes nearest to a true knowledge of himself when his need is greatest, and in knowing something of what he is and what he wants he becomes more aware of God, of the home of his spirit, and 'his heart is uneasy until it shall rest in Him'. Love, we know, is realized at parting, but the trouble is that many are too content with what is given to them in the visible and temporal order of the world and know not that in this preoccupation with what seems substantial and is really passing they are bidding adieu to what seems unsubstantial and is everlasting. Wonder and admiration of the invisible, which form the prelude of true religion, are destroyed by the commonplace and by prosperity and God has to wait until the soul cries out of the depths, 'because with the Lord is mercy and plentiful redemption'. Thus it is through darkness that the soul is driven to the light and has a glimpse of God's grandeur and goodness by contrast with its own state.

This natural religion is, we may be sure, abetted by God, and those of good will can always be sure of His grace. It is nevertheless far different from the revelation of Christ. Truth is seen through the mirror of human reflection and human experience, and though the portrait, as the early fathers of the Church observed with alarm, has a resemblance to the doctrines of Christianity, and though anthropologists love to emphasize this resemblance, it is but superficial as an image seen in water compared with the original. We may ask, nevertheless, to what heights does this natural religion reach. The answer must be tentative because God, being free, can exalt what is human to the plane of His own love, and therefore there may well be exceptions to the law I have stated. The mind of man is limited by the nature of its possessor, for it is not the mind which thinks but man. The result of this is writ large in the history of thought and human opinion. There is a body of truth, a kind of common denominator to the infinite variety of view which has been expressed in every age. There is scarcely a subject which has not been in dispute, God and His nature, the spiritual world, the soul, the body, free will, thought, sensation, colour, shape, time and space, life and matter, and yet every generation is sure that truth to some extent is there before it and waiting for its statement. And despite all checks we advance in knowledge and we live by certain truths which it would be suicidal for us to deny. The explanation, in short, of this is that like fish in a deep sea we live in an environment which blurs truth; our senses make definite what otherwise is abstract, and alas! our senses are incapable of picturing to themselves the exact nature of what is not sensible. Our character, too, imposes its own limitations on what we perceive and think, for we never stop interpreting whatever comes before our vision. Only the pure of heart see God, the Scripture tells us, and by 'pure', for the moment, let us mean freedom from prejudice, self-seeking and immature judgment. When we think of the invisible, we are bound to reduce it to a level which suits us, to represent it to ourselves by shape and colour and symbol or leave it vague and abstract, a hollow form with a minimum of content. To children abstract words mean very little, and even to the wise they are tantalizing, because they hide as much as they convey. So irritating is this infirmity of ours that many refuse to acknowledge any truth in these abstractions, and they are followed by those religious people who deny the validity of reason in religion and fall back upon some ineffable experience. But reason can and should be used as a handmaid, and the Christian revelation does not disdain its help. In natural religion man's mind is busy, but in thinking of the invisible and the goal of all his desires he is like a blind man reading braille. He learns of God and has a kind of blind contact with Him. Then with all the means available he slowly constructs a true but abstract and cold intellectual image of this living deity, and mainly by negative terms he is able to describe it as infinite and unchanging and without flaw. Here his philosophy stops and religious wisdom takes up the tale, and out of its own indigence the soul calls God its plenitude and longs for Him as its end, its love and its being. Errors can, however, creep in here because the way in which the indigence is felt is varied, and desire following on this will fill up the abyss of God with the characteristics it needs. God may become too human or again too remote from all that is associated with the agony of human striving. He is curtained in darkness or exposed as an idol.

This, then, be our theory of the human intellect what it may, is the experience of human thinking in history and practice. The history of religion and philosophy shows that the mind can suffer from vertigo and is not at ease on the heights. The mind is always being pulled down to the familiar and has to aid itself with images from the visible and the tangible, and moreover, the mind is constantly the victim of the soul's desires, and thinks as it feels and wills. Thus the man who was created after God's image begins to create God after his own image, and when he leaves the everyday world he knows, and travels in thought above himself, his thought becomes more and more rarefied and he is in danger of confusing what are totally opposite, what is mere emptiness with fullness of being, surcease from care with the repose of infinite activity and the radiance of God's abounding goodness with the cold vanishing point of human knowledge. So miserable has been the story of man's intercourse with the true God that we might guess that God must in His generosity have helped man to a better knowledge and provided some authentic revelation of Himself. That this has happened is the claim of Christianity, which boldly declares that it is the teacher and guardian of good tidings, the revealer of God in His truth and love. Not only is our natural reason guided to understand clearly what is within its own compass but a new path is opened up which man himself could not trace, and the end of this is a divine sonship in union with the Son of God, Jesus Christ.[1]

Here is the step from natural religion to supernatural revelation, and we must now examine the content of this revelation, God's way of communicating it and man's reaction to this gift. It is at this point, as I have said, that variation in opinion will naturally show itself. The true con-

[1]During the period when human science was in an exalted mood and a comparative study of religion seemed to show that the highest cults and the Christian faith were of the same pattern and differed only in degree, it became the fashion to deny the distinction between the natural and the supernatural or revealed. It was even asserted that God was immanent or expressed in man, and that, as 'in God we live and move and have our being', so God lived and had His being in us and (only in a more aristocratic sense) also in Christ. These views belonged to the liberalistic and idealistic philosophy of the period, and with its passing they too have suffered the fate they deserved. The check which science has suffered, the new scientific modesty so noticeable in the writings, for example, of Einstein, Eddington, Russell and Lindemann, and a more profound study of the so-called likenesses in religious cults, have freed us from this error. What the Catholic faith proclaims may, perhaps, be suspected as too high to be true, but that its Logos is God's and not man's is certain. Man has never invented such good news, and it is inconceivable that he could have thought out for himself the relationship of the Divine Being with himself and with a human nature such as Christ possessed; nor again has he ever been able to state for himself how man remaining man could share in the divine life and love. Not a single step in the development of Christian theology is possible without supernatural faith, and, as soon as this supernatural help is discarded, the theology or philosophic

clusion will be prejudged if already an error has been committed in the analysis of the power of the human mind. Looking back on the past and what are present tendencies, two such errors confront us. They are both extremes and in contradiction with each other. The first says that no sphere of reality lies outside the compass of the human mind; the second denies the competence

interpretation ceases to be luminous, as the bar of an electric stove turns grey when the current is turned off. One is reminded of the story of the Chinese Emperor and the nightingale.

A quite different question concerns the intimate relation of particular privileged souls with God outside Christianity. Christianity claims to be the covenanted way of union between the world and God. God has declared that His forgiveness and love are to be found in 'the way, the truth and the life'— Christ and the Body of which He is the Head. By this doctrine Christianity stands or falls, but it does not exclude the probability of uncovenanted graces. If experience be taken as a test, it would appear that God has been very bountiful with these graces, but judgment here can be nothing but idle conjecture, as God has withheld from us knowledge of His dealings with individual souls. 'What is that to thee? Follow thou me.' He has revealed to the world His will that all should be incorporated in Christ and so become one family, of one body and one spirit; and it is the duty of those who believe in Christianity to invite all to this supper of the Lamb. If others are fed who have not entered, and if they appear to show the same divinized features as the saints of the household, we can surmise that they have been in some way christened. That is all. But only the greatest confusion is caused, if on the strength of this belief the division between God's royal, supernatural gift of Himself as He is and natural perfection is blurred.

of the human mind either in the realm of the supernatural or the suprasensible or in both. The first has this result, that the supernatural is treated with suspicion and the word of God is subjected to human judgment in precisely the same way as any other news, information or discovery, so that the final outcome of this error is the total denial of the transcendent. The methods employed in the physical sciences gave this error a long innings during the nineteenth century, and its failure came when a number of philosophers and scientists pointed out that this form of rationalism was unable to account for the most obvious facts of our experience, qualities, time, growth and personality. Poincaré went so far as to question the comfortable beliefs of physical scientists even within their own domain. Their science is built on airy hypotheses which can be changed at will, and there is no *terra firma*, no indubitable aerodrome from which the flight in thought takes its rise. A host of facts were then brought to light to confirm this inadequacy of the supposedly most certain of mental activities, and the consequence was a rush to the opposite error. If we are unable to know nature, if our knowledge of ourselves is so dark, is it not clear that our knowledge of the transcendent and what pertains to God must be still more precarious? A new error thus was promulgated which denied the validity of human reason in religion, and above all in the presence of a divine revelation.

The truth, as may be surmised, must lie somewhere between these two extremes, and in order that it may be seen, certain distinctions are required. It does not follow that because the sphere of the supernatural must be above human contemplation, man is altogether at a loss, still less that our knowledge of the world around us is thereby made suspect. It would seem that our mind helped out by our senses is equal to the task of making certain broad distinctions and advancing slowly to further knowledge about nature. This must be so, for otherwise our criticism of ourselves and our powers would be itself an illusion and we should have no knowledge even of the meaning of an illusion. Moreover, a modicum of knowledge of what transcends our sensible faculties and our immediate perceptions is required, for we must be able to stand apart from ourselves and our activities to be able to judge their worth. Such judgment postulates fixed standards, and, if again all knowledge is not to be an illusion, these standards must hold good for reality as a whole as well as for our own intellectual satisfaction. There is, therefore, a sphere of the suprasensible which is attainable by the human mind, and this fact once and for all guarantees reason in its search for ultimate causes and for God. How far the mind can thus proceed will be a matter of experience, and experience has indeed shown clearly where the limitation lies. The mind *qua* mind has no limits to it, and this means that what it says must be true, however veiled or shortsighted it may be for some cause or other. That it is veiled and shortsighted is equally clear in experience, and the explanation of this is readily forthcoming. It is not the mind which thinks but man, and a man is made up of body as well as soul. Hence the thought will always be by and in the medium of something which veils it and checks it. I think of some object and, in order to understand it, I have to work upon it by means of sensible data. Even with regard to myself I carry with me a number of portraits and memories, and these are built upon the fundamental activities which give a permanent, substantial theme to the melodies which are constantly changing. I do not know myself as I am; I know that I am, and what I am is far more than I can grasp in consciousness, and to the grave I shall remain this odd creature who has to discover himself and grow into being what he ought to be. My knowledge then is my glory and my defeat; it is the test of all and the percipient of nothing by itself; it lives for truth and has to utter that word in the abstract and run to the senses to escape boredom. Not only this. As each human being is more than his mind and grows by following his desires, the mind is constantly a captive of those desires and serves them like a djinnee in a bottle. *Pondus meum amor meus.* I assimilate myself to what I love; what is little is lifted up to greatness by my desire and may be falsely adored, as a child maternally fondles the doll in its arms, or God is brought low and made to correspond with our soiled and all too human knowledge.

If such be the condition of our human knowledge, we can understand why the pendulum of human experience swings, now to excessive assurance in human knowledge, and then to a profound, if passing, disbelief in it and up to the religion of the heart, and we can interpret and estimate the recurring phases in religion, the continual seesaw, by its standard. At present we meet both phases, and we are justified in thinking that reason must have a part, modest though that will be, in religious truth. We are not, however, out of the wood yet, as we have to settle more definitely the *rôle* of reason, and not only in relation to natural religion but to revelation. The many conflicting views on the function of authority, the progressiveness of revelation and the rights of private judgment and reason arise from uncertainty here.

The reason in man works with the aid of the senses and is stimulated to activity by desire. An old half-truth would have it that the mind is a kind of mirror of reality, that a number of impressions are made on it and reproduced. This crude explanation has this of truth, that the senses and the mind are to some extent passive, but while we are not at liberty to perceive and think what we like, we are nevertheless also interiorly active throughout the process of knowing. Our senses are active in the selection of their data and form them into a pattern, in accordance usually with the external world, and the mind is actively engaged on these apparitions of the real, translating them and reading into them the meaning which they convey. It is the mind which discerns the meaning and order and distinction of things, as a sea voyager makes out on the misty horizon the shape of land, and it is ever striving to call them by their proper names, to see how and why they are what they are and interrelated, and what are the ultimate reasons for their constitution. But while it forms to itself ideas of things and how they are interconnected—and in this is interiorly active—it cannot act arbitrarily. It is subject to the laws of nature and the laws of thought which it did not make. There is then activity and passivity in the act of knowledge, and that knowledge is linked up with sense experience and can advance beyond sense experience only with the help of memory and imagination. Human beings are not the makers of truth and beauty; they have to discover them, and they can do so because they are the infants of the spiritual kingdom, able to understand what is told them and to put together the information, but dependent all their lives on sense, on belief and on abstract principles.

If this be true, then there is clearly an ambiguity in the expression 'free thought'. Reason is active, but truth is imposed from without and is assented to from within, and there can clearly be no free thought if by that is meant the right or power to decide by human authority or according to personal wishes what shall be true or false. As, however, the assent to truth is felt to be peculiarly our own—and I have shown how active the mind is in forming to itself a true idea of the external world—the sense of the words may well be freedom from external compulsion. We cannot think as we like, but we should be allowed to think for ourselves, so far as that is possible. Education is based on this principle. Children are taught to think for themselves, and we honour the man who communicates to the world some truth which he has himself discovered. Moreover we live in conditions in which certainties are rare and opinions are rife. It is good that opinions should be tested and not swallowed, even though the daily papers seem to show as a result that certainties are treated as opinions and opinions as dogmas. Where there is so much uncertainty each should be left with his freedom to choose which side he may prefer. That is the ideal. In practice every State and every family and institution knows that there are actions and views which cannot be tolerated, and if they are wise they know, too, as the Gospel so clearly indicates, that the multitudes must be well taught and directed by habits to what is true and uplifting. This means that in practice beliefs must be continually imposed on a willing people who discern vaguely but surely, even if they do not and cannot fully understand, what is to their good.

Human wisdom then depends upon a conjoined activity and passivity in our thinking. It is free in the sense that each mind ideally should discover truth for itself and be ready to accept the laws of life and nature and the wisdom which is the inheritance of the ages. But it is an observed fact, and the fact gives rise to many problems, that interest and sympathy and desire play a large part in all knowledge. Desire is present in everything we do and think, and it is above all active when truth is also valuable. We are not likely, save in the interests of some philosophic system, to quarrel over the multiplication table, but the world has been divided from the beginning of time on every matter which touches the heart, as witness now the warring convictions on politics and religion, on asceticism, sacraments, common worship and liturgy, reason and faith, humility, casuistry, fascists, communists, Buchmanites and the Catholic Church. At the end of the nineteenth century, in the revolt against rationalism, an appeal was made to the famous saying of Pascal that the heart has its reasons which the reason cannot know, and a new phase of an old philosophy came into prominence which placed love or acquaintance or intuition above the abstractions of scientific knowledge.

Theoretically and ideally the mind must always have the primacy over the other human activities, and therefore the last word. In fact, however, as we must recognize, interest and love can act as substitutes for the reason and at times outrun it. We recognize this in morals when we make children and those without proper intellectual training love the good, and most are prepared to admit that in human relationships love may not need long arguments and careful apologies. An apprehension of some kind must precede the longing and so give sight to it, but it may be very dim, and then by mutual help, as knowledge gives the desire more fuel to inflame it and love intensifies the knowledge, the two should bring that loving understanding which is the ideal state for man. Too often, alas! one or other usurps power and creates prejudices and falsehoods or the cold and narrow criticism which misses the truth. It is hard to know

208

which is the more dangerous error. The self-satisfaction of the scholar can be an abominable vice and in the lecture room he can finger ideas which are winged with death. On the other hand, the hot violence of prejudice can be equally destructive. Alone perhaps in the depths whence conscience issues is there an incorruptible love, for there is something in each man which must match him and all he would be with that alone which can give joy to his heart and being; and just as in art men measure their work by some standard dimly apprehended which leaves them dissatisfied with the best they have done, and as men and women at a crisis or turning of the road of life cry out 'For this have I lived!' so too in regard to truth and to love there is always something or someone who sways their souls to an as yet uncomprehended peace. And it is in the light of this that we must now study revelation and its effect and demands upon man.

The analysis I have given concerns natural knowledge and the objects which fall within its scope, and we have seen that the ideal is for man to understand it by a reason which is both active and passive and with the aid of desire, and we have also ground for believing that the altitudes of God will in fact, if not necessarily, always be obscure. Because of this obscurity we can argue that God is likely to aid man with some revelation of Himself, and this antecedent probability is confirmed by Christianity, which claims to be the genuine revelation of God and to surpass infinitely all that man could know and appreciate of his own effort. Let us assume that this is true,[1] and accept the official and traditional version of revelation. According to this God became man that 'man', as an early writer wrote, 'might become God' or to put the essence of Christianity in an exact formula: Revelation is the good news of eternal life in Jesus Christ. God, that is, speaks directly to man in His beloved Son and reveals to the world of Jew and Gentile a way and a truth

[1] I have to make this assumption in this short paper. To prove it would take a book. St. John wrote his Gospel to prove 'that Jesus is the Christ, the Son of God, and that believing you may have life in His name'. He therefore wrote of the signs 'that Jesus did in the sight of His apostles'. These signs consisted of the great miracles worked during His lifetime and the supreme fact of the Resurrection. St. Paul and the early Church used this same argument, and they knew what Christ had claimed to be. This claim appeared to His disciples, Jews and monotheists though they were, to be undeniable. His character and teaching were holy and authoritative as only God could be. The centuries have confirmed this belief. To those of us who live so far away in time from the years of Christ's ministry certain facts stand out. The first is that the figure of Christ could not have been invented by the evangelists; the story does not read like a fairy tale; it does not omit strange details; it is not credulous. But in that story the teaching, the character and the miracles run together into an inseparable whole, and, what is more, the passion and death are so real as to make the reader at first stupefied by the tale of the

and a life which makes all who accept it the sons
of God and sharers in the divine nature. The
revelation is communicated with absolute divine
authority; it is to be accepted on that divine
authority and if obeyed it will exalt man through
grace into a life of thought and love which is
beyond his conceiving; and if rejected the loss will
mean the deprivation of God's love for ever.

Before expanding the content of this 'good
news' we may note certain points which bear on
man's receptiveness of it. Christ speaks with
authority as God, and therefore as truth itself. He
speaks also as love incarnate and as proposing in

Resurrection, and only on second thought to see how that
Resurrection is the keynote of the whole story. Secondly, Christ
is distinct from every other founder of a religion and from every
other saint or mystic in His assertion of boundless authority and
the right to rule of Himself the hearts and lives of men. Thirdly,
all other religions have arisen out of great civilizations and are
marked with their temporal characteristics; Christ is neither Jew
nor Gentile but the voice which can command the obedience
of every man's love. Finally, His last testament is an institution
which has broken every law of historical bodies, surviving the
natural periods of vigour and decline, and surviving without any
change in its form or character. By the continued existence of the
Church Christ has outmanoeuvred time and is able to speak to
each generation as present to it and raise it from death to eternal
life. For the evidence of this set of truths there are innumerable
books. I suggest the appropriate articles in the *Dictionnaire de
Théologie, Le Dogme de la Trinité* by J. Lebreton, *Jesus Christ*
by L. de Grandmaison, *The Everlasting Man* by G. K. Chester-
ton, and *Christ in the Church*.

His wisdom what is for the eternal good of man. It follows that what he says is different from any human statement. It bears the stamp of divinity and all interpretation of it must be such that it leaves intact the original word or is itself guaranteed by the author to be a faithful transcript and development of it. If once uncertainty were to arise as to the essential meaning of that message, then the divine quality of it would have disappeared, like Eurydice, from the grasp of man. This divine character or quality will appear not only in the authority with which the message is taught, but also in the contents of it. It is like the Logos which issuing from the Godhead returns there; it is a plan which is not a providence for man as man, but for man as potentially by grace made like to God Himself in Jesus Christ. The consequences of this are that revelation must be mysterious as concerning an end which is above human ideals, that it will contain truths about God's nature which no human mind will ever be able to fathom, that the way of life will have therefore to be accepted by faith in God's word and promise and that the human mind will have to be illuminated so as to perceive the divine character in the good news. This illumination is by what theologians call grace, and without it there will be lacking that intuitive sympathy which in other fields, as we know, makes all the difference between a successful and unsuccessful interpreter of a manuscript or work of art or novel work of philosophy. What happens in human relations is that something clicks in our minds, the pieces fall into pattern, and our sympathetic efforts are rewarded by possession of the mind of the author. This is what St. Paul means by 'having the mind of Christ', and as Christ thought 'it not robbery to claim an equality with God', our poor frail souls have to be uplifted into an order of equality with Christ that we may accept Him and know His will. The change is brought about by grace, which acts as a transforming power and salutes the inhabitation of the Holy Spirit, the seal of union.

When instructing His disciples, Christ told them that they should listen to the teaching of those who sat upon the chair of Moses, though they should not imitate their works. He himself was the rightful occupant of that chair, and His authority was divine and His truth heavenly. In this He is different from all other teachers, and hence the attitude of believers in Him must be different. We have seen what the normal procedure of the human mind is, its relation to fact, to authority and to desire. There are those who would keep that attitude unchanged, and there is a school which would change everything and make an entirely new start, in the experience of faith. The first is the liberal and modernist outlook, the

213

second is the apocalyptic one. Both surely contain elements of truth which can be reconciled. At first, before faith has been given, a man should approach the problem of his destiny and the Christian answer to it with sympathy and fairness of mind. There will be few who have not some antecedent prejudices which it is the task of a reasonable apologetic to remove. That apologetic will, if it be wise, set forth the credentials of Christianity and show how the mind should move logically from the existence of God to the need of help from Him to achieve happiness in Him. It will examine historically the claims of Christ and the work He came to do, and the Church He founded to continue His teaching. What degree of conviction can be reached at the end of this stage will always be a matter of dispute, but it suffices to say here that the evidence when seen with the eyes of faith is final. I do not mean by that that it remains unreasonable without faith. To say that would be to misunderstand the meaning of faith. Faith does not act on the will alone; it principally enlightens the mind to see, and to see what is there already under a new aspect. What is given in the very act looks boundlessly reasonable and compels the whole man, and it is backed up by all that went before. It has been said of the centurion at the foot of the cross that he saw a man suffering and recognized God. The two thieves beheld the same behaviour, but for the one it was transfigured and became the redemptive act of a God; and similarly when the two disciples on the way to Emmaus had their faith brought back to them by their fellow traveller, they saw that they had been blind to what had been there all the time. They had missed the evidence, which scripture as well as the manner of their companion presented. 'Did it not behove the Son of Man to suffer . . .?'

Up to the point of faith, therefore, a man must act normally, and after it there is a change. Like Thomas the doubter he falls at the feet of Christ and cries: 'My Lord and my God!' and in this cry there is complete surrender and the beginning of a new life. It is perfectly true that the old things have passed away and that all is now seen in the grey morning light of a day which is God's without end. The rationalist is wrong in not recognizing this. There is a complete severance from the past in the initial act which makes man a divine being instead of a human one. This must be so. Grace transforms, and as in physical changes there is the crackle and hiss when one form dies to become another, so in the death of an old man and the putting on of the new there are pangs and self-renunciations which are inevitable. It is this fact which scandalizes those who are rich in mind or talents or noble ambitions. They hold that God cannot intend to take away that most precious of gifts wherewith, in its proper exercise, God is most honoured by man. They are shocked, and despise the act of total surrender as an act of cowardice, and spurn the act of authority which demands it as wanton and oracular. They are not, however, true to the highest instinct of man which makes him in love give his all and keep nothing back. In all love stories faith is tried in the fire, and the hero, though he cannot turn to one Who 'has the words of eternal life', does not fail because of a 'hard saying'. If this be so between a man and a maid, it must be the law of love between God and man. There is in man that inner source of pride and strength which I have described as 'interior activity' and under the name of 'free thought'. It asserts itself in private judgment and makes a man a personality among his fellows with rights and liberty. No human being can rob us of this privilege, and it is so much part and parcel of ourselves that it may not cross our minds that we could be asked to surrender it. And yet unless we do, when divine love would draw us to its own being, we keep back the one gift requisite. God empties Himself of His divine glory for our sake, and we refuse to empty ourselves of what is our most cherished human excellence to become like to Him. And so love fails and the grace of transformation is inoperative and we do not change our name and being into Christ. That is the failure which the apocalyptic school has understood, and it would be easy to show how this is responsible for the constant attempt to attenuate the authority of Christ, to confuse His divinity and to cut the one abiding word of God into human patterns and judgments which have no finality and vary with the spirit of the age.

It is no wonder that religious minds sensible of the awful distance of God from man, of His condescension in Christ, and of the sacrosanct and divine quality to be attributed to His actions and words, should fence off revelation from all human interference. In so doing they contradict the error of rationalism, but they are in danger of indulging in an extreme themselves. As in the old controversies of grace heresy kept coming in because of the temptation to attribute all to God or all to the human will, so in defiance of the Pelagianism, which gives too much to man, a modern school has taken all from man and placed salvation entirely in the divine action by grace. This truly religious attitude rings so true that it may easily pass without question. It is nevertheless defective through ignorance of the bounty of God. In the worldwide act of religion, namely, sacrifice, a victim is chosen and offered to God. That victim symbolizes the best that man can offer, which in a developed community will be himself, and it is made over to God in homage and in hope of friendship or reconciliation. The rationalist attitude, as we have seen, had the defect that it kept back the most prized object for sacrifice; the apocalyptic view does not fail here, for it hands over all to God, and makes of the divine action the whole of religion. But it forgets that sacrifice has another culmination, which consists in the divine acceptance of the offering and the handing it back to be, if the object allows of it, the food of the people. By this generosity of God what has been surrendered is restored. So likewise, though it be true that in the acceptance of revelation the authority of God takes the place of all else and man surrenders himself to grace and is taken up into a new life, nothing is really lost. In that new life, *vita abscondita in Christo*, God is all in all. He is the principle and the end; He is the life of the soul, but the old is redintegrated or orientated, and the reason and the will are not less active but newly charged.

What then happens is this, that love runs ahead of knowledge and summons it to climb heights which look cold and inhuman. Reason removes fears and obstacles in the way and so, like the ancient pedagogue, leads the learner to the school of Christ. The Incarnation and the Redemption being living facts, and the evidence of the divine authority and truth being ever externally present in the Church, the soul 'comes and sees'. This act of assimilation or response, call it what one may, is made possible by grace, which makes that to be visible and desirable as an end which is properly the *terra incognita* of God's own light and love. In this light, which is because of its omnipotence also darkness to man now, the self surrenders and obedience comprises the first law. 'Unless the seed fall into the ground it shall not have life.' But once that assent of faith is made, never to be withdrawn, the intellect realizes that it is not stultified but invigorated. It has no longer a private judgment but a filial judgment; it is no longer at the mercy of every wind of doctrine. Fastened to truth it has the task of making all that is sing together with revelation.

This, if we look back upon the intellectual and artistic achievement of Christianity, has in fact always been its object. We can note how the creator of western theology, St. Augustine, once faith had come to him, proceeded to think out its terms in filial delight; or we can watch how the Christian mind first proceeded to make clear to itself the unsearchable riches of its Master, pondering for centuries on how to express His natures and personality, His relation with the Father and the Holy Spirit. Then it turned to His work in the individual soul, and built up the theology of grace and of the Eucharist, the while its philosophers ransacked the world to make a system worthy of the name of Christ. In doing this they were quick to see that the overarching wisdom given to them in the Word helped all human activities, and especially reason. Reason and revelation, however different their ambit, had the same object, truth. Consequently Christianity, as expressed in the Church, did not decline to treat with the world. It was to be a leaven, and a myriad problems awaited it which concerned it and society and the individual. The fundamental relations between the Church and human society were marked from the beginning, but as it has taken Europe centuries to evolve its own ideas of the State and classes and corporations and liberty and democracy, it may well be that the ever growing context of Christ will embrace these still secular elements. The steady development of theology from the first contents of revelation, the Trinity and Incarnation, through grace and the Sacraments, the Mother of God and His saints to the nature and workings of the Church, indicates that its sweep will in time take in society and the physical universe. We know that all is to be re-capitulated in Christ and we have precious indications of the function of nature under its new cosmic Head in St. Paul—in his saying that the whole world travails to the revelation of the Son of God and in the texts which refer to the 'elements of the world'. The possibility of such a development shows how false it is to separate off the Word of God from all that man discovers by the light of his natural reason. The filial attitude born in faith makes more constant and sure the efforts of scientist and philosopher. The meaning of morals has been deepened by the news of man's new dignity and God's love; life has grown more sacred and marriage has become the symbol of the eternal union of Christ with His Church, and in turn the truths of the natural order, as more familiar to us and intelligible, serve as a medium whereby to understand and enjoy the Gospel and the Creeds.

These examples will show how in faith obedience to the word of God and reason can work together. The authoritative character of revelation must remain intact and be continued in the Church which speaks in Christ's name. The Church must teach, and in that sense, in being faithful to its mission, it is oracular. But it is an oracle which does not dismiss reason and love as out of place. It relies on Scripture and the ever living continuity of its saints and teachers for its decisons. Where revelation is not concerned, it leaves free the cut and thrust of human opinion and hypothesis unless the conclusions scandalize the little ones of Christ and imperil their faith. That it should at times appear harsh and ungenerous to individuals and their speculations is due to its sad experience of the past. Too often have tares been sown in the night, and it is natural and logical that the Church should, as the steward of Christ, prefer to be thought narrow-minded than risk the loss of one soul for whom its Lord died. This care and discipline will, however, vary in different ages according to the general sanity or insanity of an age, and in a serene epoch there would be little check on freedom. In matters of revelation, on the other hand, the method of reasoning is not that of the physical sciences. In science, as I have already said, the reason begins with sensible experience and by multiplying this experience naturally and artificially is able to arrive at an hypothesis. This method is, however, not so suitable to the truths of philosophy, and the method which is appropriate to revelation is closer to that of philosophy.

To understand this we must return to the definition already given of the content of faith, viz., the good news of eternal life in Christ. This new life appeals to the will with an urgency which cannot be neglected, and so desire gives wheels to the mind to make it run with the demand made upon the self. The understanding is, however, always in the rear and knows revelation to be a life or death concern of the soul before it dwells upon the articles of belief. These articles are abstract, and, unlike natural knowledge, have not their

origin in sense experience. They are truths which
are believed on divine authority, and it takes time
to appreciate their import and unity. Grace which
is the cause of holiness enables us to appropriate
them, and it is by our growing identification with
Christ that His thoughts and His will lose their
abstract character, melt and become home truths.
Thus it is that we pass from the love of Christ to
His dogmas and back again from the meditation
of His dogmas to a deeper and deeper realization
of both Christ and the creeds. In philosophy we
work out what we already know, and each generation works afresh upon the most familiar facts and
experiences, knowing and loving, choice, sensation, objects, persons and God. The method is to
use the wisdom of the past and ponder over what
is already in some sense before us. This habit of
contemplation is different from the scientific
method and unsuited to the field of science; it
requires an object before us which is so rich as to
merit absorbed attention, and its riches need
deciphering and separating off from all that clings
to it and is confused with it. It would seem that,
given human nature as it is, time is a necessary
function in the understanding of such objects, and
perhaps, too, the human mind, because of its
weakness, will proceed dialectically, saying too
much and then saying too little, and moving down
the road by swerving from one side to the other.

Human beings do not escape their fate and avoid error even after God has revealed His truth to them. But that truth is never lost and abides in Christ's mystical Body, the Church. There its beauty awaits the contemplation of every age, so ancient and so ever fresh, and the doctrine of the Church develops when the inexhaustible riches of that truth become more and more apparent as the Kingdom of God grows and Christ reaches to His full stature. Christ is the beginning and end of revelation. It is He Who is known better by being saluted as the Son of God and the Son of man, as the high priest and victim of love on Calvary, as the way and the truth and the life. He is seen again in the doctrines of grace and the communion of saints and the dogma of God's motherhood, and He is seen in the doctrine of the Church as the Mystical Body. As the vine with vinebranches, as the firstborn of a new race, as the head with many members, as the Eucharist which makes us into a new paste, as the bridegroom with His bride, as love which transforms mankind into an identity with itself, so that we are all one in Christ and incorporated, He brings all His doctrines into the splendour of His love. To know God as He is, is the end of the supernatural life and the promise of revelation, and it is by adhesion to the sublime doctrines which are exclusively His own that we are made like to Him.

VI

By the Rev. Prof. WALTER M. HORTON

The idea of revelation is the expression of man's desperate need of light upon the ultimate meaning and purpose of his existence, and his faith that though human wisdom is unable to find the needful light, it may be bestowed from on high, by the mercy of God, whose eternal wisdom for ever struggles to overcome the dark incomprehension of His creatures.

Such an idea could never cross the mind of a perfectly contented creature, harmoniously adapted to his world. Contentment and self-complacency are the deadly enemies of faith in revelation; humility and self-distrust are its natural preconditions. It is not to be wondered at that trust in divine revelation wanes with the establishment of self-sufficient systems of civilization, and waxes again with their decay. In a static society (*e.g.*, China before Sun Yat-sen) whose settled customs and institutions are based upon accepted presuppositions about the meaning of life, it may appear that nothing more than a sound system of transmissive instruction is needed to guide men to their true destiny. In a rapidly expanding culture (*e.g.*, Europe before 1914) where new discoveries and inventions continually unsettle the good old ways, the sense of security is less complete, but the sense of progress may still keep men self-sufficient. 'Yes, we are young and ignorant,' they say, 'but we are learning fast, and tomorrow may stumble upon the philosopher's stone. Yes, there are disturbing disharmonies and deficiencies in our life, but things may be better just around the next corner. We have conquered many perils in our physical environment, and overcome many evils in our social order, by our own courage and clear thinking; why should we not solve the whole human problem by continuing along the same lines? Why should we throw up our hands and cry for help when the goal is in sight, and no supernatural rescuer is clearly in evidence?'

Such words have a brave sound while the fabric of civilization still holds firm, and the agencies of culture still push on aggressively. Most of us can remember the time when this Gospel of Self-Reliance carried with it such prestige as to make some religious thinkers quail before it, disclaiming all intention of humbling the human will, or setting limits to the powers of the human mind. Today, in most parts of the world, the situation is radically altered. It is becoming evident that we are at the end of the period of expanding European culture which has lasted since the Renaissance, and at the beginning of a period of confusion and retrenchment which must last until some new principle of order emerges, upon which a new civilization can be based. In the face of this disquieting prospect, men's moral and intellectual self-assurance is deserting them. Human reason and human will power are once more at a discount, as in similar crises before; and *the danger now is, not that divine revelation will be spurned, but that it will be embraced with fanatical fervour, and understood in a superstitious sense.*

It is not the place of the Christian Church to spread panic fear in times of defeat, in order that men may run into her sheltering arms as a last desperate resort. It is beneath her dignity to take strategic advantage of human weakness in its hour of humiliation, as it is beneath her dignity to bow before human might in its hour of exaltation. One eternal Gospel she has to proclaim, in fair weather and foul; and if the tone of her proclamation must needs vary with the times, it should vary *inversely*, not directly. The time for warning admonitions about the insufficiency of human wisdom, and the need of superhuman light, was when Science sat enthroned as queen of the Western world, ruling

Africa, Asia and the Islands through her prime
ministers, Technology and Military Prowess.
Now that the course of events has made the insufficiency of human wisdom all too plain, the time
has come for a word of encouragement and hope,
such as only the Church can give: the Good News
concerning the revealed Word and Will of God,
which are light and not darkness, indwelling
power and not overmastering might; which demand no *sacrificium intellectus*, no cringing servitude of the will, but raise up and glorify all human
senses and faculties till they are adequate for the
crisis that must be faced—adequate not in themselves, but through the enduement and indwelling
of divine light and strength.

I. REVELATION AND REASON IN THE EARLY CHURCH AND THE REFORMATION

The Church should know how to proclaim the
Good News of divine revelation in such a time as
this, for at least twice before she has led the
Western world through similar periods, trium-
phantly; once in the early days of her history,
when Graeco-Roman civilization had experienced
a 'failure of nerve' and was slowly disintegrating,
and once again at the time of the Reformation,
when mediaeval feudal society was being rent
asunder by new and explosive forces, carrying

down in its collapse the ecclesiastical system which had been so closely united with it. In both of these periods, the Church's claim to possess light from above revealed by God Himself, was like an enheartening bugle call amid the confusion of the times, which stayed the rout and allayed the fears of those who rallied to her standard. It did not humiliate human reason; it saved panic-stricken men from fanaticism and superstition, and it eventually saved all that was best in the decadent secular culture of the time as a part—subordinate but valuable—of the body of Christian teaching.

The pagan civilization into which the Christian message first came was one which could look back upon great achievements, but was no longer sure of itself. The Greek world could boast of the cultural achievements of the age of Pericles, and the philosophy of Plato and Aristotle. The Roman world could boast of the military skill which had conquered the whole Mediterranean basin, and the political genius which had introduced law and order throughout the conquered area, while respecting the special customs of different peoples. But these distinguished achievements had not brought peace to men's souls, nor enabled them to face the ultimate questions of life with equanimity. There was a general feeling that life was a voyage upon rough and uncharted waters, which no frail human barque could hope to navigate, unless . . .

What had Plato said . . . 'Unless any of us may find a safer and less risky course upon the steadier craft of some divine message.'[1]

Agreed upon the necessity of 'some divine message', men disagreed as to where it was to be found. Some found guidance in the time-honoured usage of oracles and auspices, or in the popular cult of astrology; but there were those who doubted the validity of all such 'revelations'. Others found superhuman wisdom in the mystery cults, or in the ancient religions of the Orient, whose cryptic utterances possessed a certain glamour by virtue of sheer antiquity. Still others held fast to the main intellectual traditions of the West, but sought in Plato's 'myths', and in his doctrine of 'divine madness', the clue to a higher wisdom, lying beyond dialectical reason in the sphere of mystic intuition and ecstasy—a confused and perilous state of mind, in which all counsels of clear thinking and sober morality seemed likely to be swept aside by a wave of superstitious credulity and moonstruck fanaticism.

The Apostle Paul, addressing his message to a world thus hungrily questing for an authentic word from God, claims in the most unmistakable terms to possess in Christ the revelation which all are seeking. His apostleship, he says, is 'not from men, neither through man, but through Jesus

[1]*Phaedo*, 35 (Duncan's translation).

Christ, and God the Father, who raised him from the dead'.[1] His preaching is 'not in persuasive words of wisdom, but in demonstration of the Spirit and of power; that your faith should not stand in the wisdom of men, but in the power of God'.[2] Yet the revelation which Paul thus announces is quite different, as he is well aware, from the revelation which the pagan world is expecting. It is no detailed horoscope of the future—although Paul does not hesitate to venture some predictions about 'last things' and the life to come; no mystic vision of celestial principalities and powers—although Paul, too, has had his ecstatic revelations of heavenly matters; no occult theosophy unfolding cosmic mysteries too high for the unlearned to comprehend—although Paul has an esoteric teaching for those who are ready for such strong meat. It is something which is ridiculous to the erudite pagan, shocking to the orthodox Jew, and convincing only to the humble soul whom God has prepared to see it; 'the light of the knowledge of the glory of God in the face of—'[3] a defeated, humiliated, executed Man!

The light thus strangely revealed is for Paul not contrary to the light of nature and the light of conscience. God's 'everlasting power and divinity' are so clearly to be 'perceived through the things that are made', and even the Gentiles have His moral

[1] Gal. i. 1.   [2] I Cor. ii. 4, 5.   [3] II Cor. iv. 6

law so indelibly 'written in their hearts', that all men are 'without excuse'.[1] Yet as a matter of fact, the wisdom of men seems incapable of using this natural revelation aright. Lacking the humble and childlike spirit which is ready to respond to the appeal of the divine love as made known in the Crucified One, they miss the final and essential truth about God, and fall back into idolatry or immorality, incurring the divine wrath. All truth is Christ's, all will at last be found consistent with Him in Whom 'all things consist';[2] so Paul is willing to match wits with the pagans and speculate about hidden cosmic secrets, as he does in the Epistle to the Colossians. But he is convinced that the one revelation necessary to salvation, without which all human wisdom is foolishness, is something so simple and luminous that the common man can grasp it by an act of faith.

The attitude of the early Church toward secular learning and rival revelations was not at first clearly defined. Two powerful considerations pulled her in opposite directions. On the one hand, she must testify to an incredulous world that the true light was now come, in whose presence all human philosophy and all previous religious teaching seemed insufficient and misleading. On the other hand, she must not make it appear that God has contradicted Himself; that what He

[1]Rom. i. 20; ii. 15.   [2]Col. i. 17.

spoke 'to the fathers . . . by divers portions and in divers manners' is inconsistent with what He has now said to us 'in his Son'.[1]

With some early defenders of the faith, the first of these two considerations was all-determinative. In order to exalt the revelation of God in Christ, they attacked all its rivals in unmeasured terms. The virtues of the pagans were only splendid vices, their gods were demons, and any appearance of truth in their philosophy or religion was a satanic counterfeit, designed to lead the unwary astray. A few extremists, following Marcion, went so far as to include the religion of the Old Testament in this general indictment, thus setting the Christian revelation in complete opposition to everything that had been esteemed true and holy in the ancient world.

The motives of these zealous champions of Christ must not be maligned. They feared—not without cause—that if the new Light of the World should be removed from its splendid isolation and brought into harmony with pagan or Jewish ideas, its purity would be compromised, and its character as a unique divine revelation would be lost. Even in Tertullian's *credo quia absurdum*—the classical expression of this puritanical zeal in its most extreme form—there is an exceedingly important truth enshrined, which no disciple of Christ

[1]Heb. i. 1, 2.

should forget; the dialectical opposition which constantly appears between the highest earthly wisdom and that more than earthly wisdom which uttered itself in the Sermon on the Mount and the Journey to the Cross. It is characteristic of true revelation to appear where least expected, in forms that surprise and even shock the average mind. If there is nothing absurd, from the point of view of worldly prudence, in an alleged Word of God, then can it possibly be of God? And if this be so, can there be any reconciliation between divine revelation and human wisdom? Must not any attempted reconciliation be in effect a betrayal? Nevertheless, we may be glad that more moderate counsels prevailed generally in the Church; for had these extremists had their way, the opposition between Christian truth and all other forms of truth would have become absolute. Christians have enough sins against light, as it is, to confess before God; the murder of Hypatia, the destruction of the Platonic Academy, the persecution of the Jews, the persistent hostility to scientific investigation which postponed the natural development of Alexandrian science into modern science for a millennium and a half.

Already in the New Testament itself, the outlines of a more adequate doctrine of revelation are visible, especially in the Epistle to the Hebrews and the Gospel of John. In the former, it is of course the Old Testament revelation alone that is brought into relation with the revelation in Christ; but the principle here established in the case of Jewish prophecy was destined to be applied to the case of Greek philosophy; the principle, namely, that in the Old Testament we have a true but imperfect revelation, which is to the New what a symbol or 'type' is to the reality it means and foreshadows, but to which it must eventually give way. The application of this same principle to pagan wisdom was suggested by the Prologue of the Gospel of John, which interprets Christ as the incarnate Word, the concentration in a human life of the universal divine 'light that lighteth every man that cometh into the world'. Though this light 'shineth in darkness', and is not received by those on whom it shines, it represents nevertheless a general latent sense of God among all peoples.

The early Christian apologists, following out these suggestions, identify Christ with the generally diffused *Logos spermatikos*, which operated as genuinely in the Greek philosophers as in the Hebrew prophets, and even led them to the same conclusions. If the fulfilment of Old Testament prophecy in the New Testament confirms the Gospel, how much more is the Gospel confirmed by this double fulfilment. Sometimes the congruity between prophecy and philosophy is traced to a hypothetical 'borrowing' from Moses; sometimes, as in the Epistle to Diognetus, Hebrew and pagan religious thought are placed on a substantial equality, as preparations for the Gospel. Justin Martyr is particularly generous in his attitude. Christ, he says, is 'the Logos (Reason) of whom the whole human race are partakers, and those who lived according to reason (*logos*) are Christians, even though accounted atheists. Such among the Greeks were Socrates and Heraclitus, and those who resembled them.'[1] The first great systems of Christian theology, in the school of Alexandria, were based squarely upon this view. 'The Greek Philosophy', says Clement of Alexandria, 'purges the soul, as it were, and prepares it beforehand for the reception of faith, on which the Truth builds up the edifice of Knowledge.'[2] In his theology, the Hebrew Scriptures and Greek philosophy are taken as practically cognate sources for Christian teaching.

It cannot be denied that the adoption of this hospitable attitude toward pagan philosophy opened the door for all manner of confusing and corrupting influences. Particularly through the use of the allegorical method of scriptural interpretation, it became possible to read into the sacred text one's favourite speculative theories, and read out of it almost all of its original significance. The 'acute Hellenization' of which Har-

[1] *Apol.* i. 46.   [2] *Stromateis*, vii. 3.

nack so dramatically used to warn us, was no imaginary bogy; it was a deadly disease, with which the Church had to struggle earnestly, if the integrity of the Gospel was not to be altogether destroyed. Yet the attempt to bring secular wisdom and non-Christian revelation into one body of truth with the New Testament Gospel was nevertheless necessary and legitimate. It was a task beset with supreme difficulties, owing to the paradoxical and dialectical character of Christian revelation, to which we have already alluded. From Origen to St. Thomas Aquinas and the modern liberal school the characteristic failing of philosophical theology has been its love of smooth, well-rounded surfaces and harmonious proportions—whereby the angularities of the Gospel and its divine disproportion with all human measuring rods have been concealed. To those who perceive this danger, the natural remedy may seem to be the formal abjuration of all system-building, and all attempts to corroborate the Gospel in the court of human reason. But if the Gospel is indeed, as it claims, a revelation of heavenly light and truth, if it enables the believer to grasp his world at precisely the central point, and view it from just the right angle, by what difficulties and what solemn warnings can the Christian be dissuaded from the endeavour to think his world out from this central point, and discover the unity of all truth in Christ?

Abortive and imperfect as all systems of Christian theology must be, they have not been fruitless. At least in the case of ancient Graeco-Roman civilization, we can now clearly see how in the systems of Origen, Augustine and Aquinas the essential elements of truth and value which paganism contained have been preserved for posterity, by being brought into juxtaposition if not always into real unity with the revealed Truth which stands above all civilizations and above all times.

With the triumph of Christianity over ancient paganism, the tension between divine revelation and human wisdom, of which we are so conscious in the New Testament, began to relax excessively. Particularly in the church-controlled civilization of the Middle Ages, there was such continuity between church and secular learning that revelation appeared to be the natural and inevitable culmination of a train of thought which began in the humblest sciences and proceeded steadily upwards from earth to heaven. But with the breakdown of the mediaeval cultural synthesis, the tension reappeared (*e.g.*, in the philosophy of Occam) and in the teaching of the Protestant Reformers it expressed itself in an exclusive emphasis upon divine revelation, accompanied by an extreme contempt for human reason: *sola scriptura, sola gratia, sola fide*.

Moderate and reasonable souls like Erasmus,

recognizing the need of reform, shrank back before the apparent irrationalism of the Protestants. In their insistence upon the sole authority of scripture, in their doctrine of the bondage of the human will and the blindness of the human reason, the apostle of the New Learning saw nothing but fanatical obscurantism. As a matter of historical fact, however, the Protestant Reformation has issued in a great outburst of scholarly investigation, bold self-assertion and rational discussion. How can this paradox be resolved? Through the same principle which we have already seen to be implicit in the teaching of the Early Church: *the essential luminousness of divine revelation*. If the Reformers exaggerate the darkness of the human understanding beyond any of their contemporaries it is only because a great light has dawned upon them. Karl Heim is perfectly right when he declares that the distinguishing mark of Protestant piety is to be found in 'a spiritual act which is accomplished in profound solitude and complete lucidity of mind'[1] the act in which the soul, confronted by divine revelation, immediately perceives its inherent truth, so clearly that, as Luther said, its conscience is 'thirled to the Word of God', and it cannot deny what it sees, under any threat of punishment.

[1]Karl Heim, *Spirit and Truth: the Nature of Evangelical Christianity*, p. 101.

We must not attempt to make philosophers out of the Reformers. Their historic mission was to exalt divine revelation, with all possible clarity and vehemence, in an age which was sick at heart because of the failure and corruption of the great human institution which had guided the affairs of Europe for a thousand years. They did so, inevitably, with a certain one-sidedness, and were led to some shocking conclusions—double predestination and the like—which ought to warn us against trying to follow them too closely. But with their doctrine of the 'testimony of the Holy Spirit', a testimony consisting in a clear inward apprehension of the truth of scriptural revelation, they gave reason and conscience their due rights, and opened the way for liberal Protestantism's attempt to reconcile scripture with secular science. If it was thought necessary to check the alleged spiritual revelations of the Zwickau prophets by the principle that the Spirit cannot be self-contradictory and cannot inspire actions or thoughts that are contrary to inspired scripture, the 'right of private judgment' in the interpretation of scripture was nevertheless universally recognized; and this led at length to the Quaker attempt to test all scripture by the 'inner light', and the rationalist attempt to test it by the canons of logical consistency and empirical probability. The doctrine of the witness of the Spirit thus played the same *rôle* in Reformation theology that the doctrine of the Logos played in patristic theology, and prepared the way for the liberal Protestant doctrine of the unity of all truth.

Liberal Protestantism came upon the scene at a time when secular science and philosophy were advancing with great strides, and improved facilities for transportation and communication were making the religion and philosophies of India and China as familiar as those of Greece and Rome in the time of Christ. Naturally enough, it conceived its main task to be the reconciliation of Christian teaching with modern Western thought and ancient Oriental wisdom—a task even more monumental than the mediaeval attempt to reconcile the Bible and Aristotle—and, naturally enough, it tended to *thin out* its conception of the Christian Gospel in the endeavour to *stretch it out* into sympathetic accord with so many and so diverse points of view. Now that the prestige of modern Western thought and the newness of Oriental ideas are wearing away, it is easy to see how needless and how damaging were some of the compromises into which liberal Protestant theology allowed itself to be betrayed. Most serious of all was the gradual attrition of the idea of revelation itself, through constant contact with the notions of scientific *discovery* and religious *insight*, until the distinctive element in it—divine '*disclosure* of a realm of truth which cannot be apprehended by sense, or by ordinary process of thought'[1]—tended to be lost altogether. *It should be a primary concern of contemporary theology to reassert the full Christian idea of revelation in the clearest possible terms, and re-establish its supremacy in Christian teaching, while at the same time making it plain that faith in revelation does not violate that reverence for all truth which liberal Protestantism has—let us hope—made permanently a part of the Christian conscience.*

II. THE LIMITS OF REASON AND THE SUPREMACY OF REVELATION

In Liberal Protestant thought, the old clear-cut distinction between reason and revelation has been abolished, because human discovery and divine disclosure have come to be regarded as two sides of a single process. All human knowledge, including the humblest act of sense perception, is 'revelation', because it contains something objectively 'given'. All divine self-disclosure, however astonishing and dramatic, is at the same time humanly apprehended and verified, or it has failed of its purpose. 'The test of revelation is that it reveals.'

[1]Scott, E. F., *The New Testament Idea of Revelation*, p. 5. (A book to be carefully read by all who seek to understand the authentic Christian notion of revelation.)

There is great force in this view, as against any conception of revelation which ignores the subjective element in it, or denies the place of perception and reason in the process by which it is humanly apprehended. We may agree heartily with Dr. William Adams Brown's contention, in his *Pathways to Certainty*, that revelation is not a fifth way of knowing, in addition to the four familiar supplementary methods of *authority*, *intuition*, *reasoning* and *experiment*; it is 'our way of expressing our conviction that in each of the four ways God is speaking to us and that no account of His ways of revealing Himself can be complete which does not take them all in'.[1] It is particularly important, as a safeguard against subjective delusions, to recognize that authority and intuition, the more passive aspects of the mental process by which man apprehends revelation, are no more God-given than the active rational faculties by which they must be checked and controlled.

But if all human discovery can in a sense be brought under the concept of revelation, it must nevertheless be pointed out that the concept would never have been invented if the element of the 'given' had not in some special cases been infinitely more impressive than any *datum* of perception, any new scientific 'revelation', or even— the closest analogy—any communication of new

[1]Brown, *Pathways to Certainty*, p. 79.

meaning from another person can possibly be. When a man perceives a new planet, or conceives a new mathematical theory for unifying two fields of knowledge, he shouts, 'Eureka! I have found it!' When he meets the God of Grace revealed in the Cross of Christ, he bows in gratitude, and confesses, 'Thou hast found me!'

On a line[1] ranging from sense perception at one end to faith in the Word Made Flesh at the other, the lower or subjective side of the line would be more prominent at one end, the upper or objective side (the 'given') at the other. We may therefore confine the term *Reason* to one end-segment on this line, and *Revelation* to the opposite end-segment; though reason is always correlated with objective *data*, and revelation is evident only to subjective *faith*. Between these end-segments there is a debatable middle ground which may be called *general revelation*, differing from ordinary reason

		Revelation	
[1] (Sense data)	(Values)	General	Special
Science	Philosophy	(Awareness of the holy)	(Faith in divine initiative)
	Reason		

Each type of human knowledge has as its objective data not only what stands directly above it in this diagram, but also all that stands *above and to the left*. Thus, philosophy is based upon sense data and values; Christian faith is based upon sense data, values and general revelation, as well as upon special revelation.

in that it definitely involves the religious awareness of *the holy*, differing from full-fledged revelation in that it does not necessarily involve faith in the divine initiative.

Rational methods can and should be applied to the objective data of revelation; rational discoveries can and should be regarded as minor parts of divine revelation; but reason in the strict and narrow sense means *ordinary reflective thinking*, based on sense data (*science*) and appreciative valuation (*philosophy*), while revelation strictly applies only to *the intentional self-disclosure of a gracious God*, whether mediated through the religious insight of His servants the prophets, or through the activity of One in whom He personally goes out 'to seek and to save that which was lost'. We shall not lose sight of the wider meanings of our terms; but it is *reason in the narrow sense* and *revelation in its most intense significance* whose 'limits' and whose 'supremacy' we are now concerned to establish.

The limits of reason in the sphere of *science* are being marked out very clearly in our day by the scientists themselves. Each exact science, such as physics or biology, attains the precision which is its most admirable quality by a process of *abstraction*, whereby all aspects of the phenomenon in question falling outside of the narrowly defined scope of this science are allowed to drop out of the picture completely. The aspects thus ignored are

still *there*, and must be reckoned with in any finally
adequate dealing with reality; but from the special
point of view of this science they have ceased to
exist. Among the important matters thus excluded
by abstraction are all the private, individual,
unique, unrepeatable aspects of reality, which cannot be handled simply as members of a class or
instances of a general law; all judgments of meaning or value, except in so far as they are simply
taken for granted (as in economics) and treated as
though they were facts; and finally, all questions
concerning ultimate origins, ultimate destiny, and
the ultimate nature of reality as a whole. Since the
questions which most deeply concern us fall within
this excluded sphere of *ends and meanings*, and
cannot be reduced to the merely scientific problem
of *ways and means*, it is evident that man cannot
live by science alone. The plight of our scientific-
technological civilization should make this plain
today even to the man in the street, for whom the
above analysis is too subtle.

But if science cannot solve the whole human
problem, neither can *philosophy*. Philosophy takes
into consideration what science neglects. It endeavours to appreciate and evaluate all those deli-
cate overtones of reality which science loses by
abstraction; it attempts to bring the world of
meanings and values into the right relationship
with the world of laws and facts; it presses back

off surface appearances and one-sided views toward a comprehensive survey of all reality in its depths and heights. To the end that all partial and superficial views may be overcome, it scrutinizes commonly accepted concepts and axioms, so as to lay bare whatever inner contradictions and absurd implications they may contain. In this negative and critical part of its work, philosophy is successful and extremely serviceable. On its positive and constructive side, it endlessly approaches a goal which it never reaches. All the great philosophical issues that touch us most nearly are unsettled issues, which can never be brought to the point of decision by reason alone: monism and pluralism, idealism and materialism, determinism and libertarianism. To thresh these issues out, eliminating irrational extremes and narrowing down the acceptable possibilities by patient dialectic, is an indispensable discipline for those who seek to purify and guide religious thought; but saving religious insight is unattainable by these means. We need to *know now* on what object our supreme devotion should be bestowed, and what is required of us if we would serve that Object aright; philosophy can give us light upon this central religious problem —at least by destroying unworthy idols—but *too dimly* and *too late*.

The causes of the religious insufficiency of philosophy lie much deeper than the causes of the insufficiency of science. They lie, not in any deliberate limitation of aim and method, but in the nature of the human mind, moving as it does within finite bounds and darkened as it is by all manner of foolish prejudices and evil propensities.

That man is weak and easily prone to moral deviation must be agreed, even if the idea of original sin be set aside; and the effects of his moral weakness cannot be concealed in philosophy as they can in science. Scientific objectivity is reached by the elimination of the personal equation, so that a man might be totally depraved—save for the love of truth—and still a good scientist, if he adhered to the right methods; but the philosopher cannot escape the effects of his moral weakness, since it is one of the distinguishing features of his task to deal with judgments of value, which cannot but go astray without sound moral insight. The morally twisted person cannot correctly see the saving truth without which he cannot be delivered from his twist.

But waiving the moral difficulty, there remains the fact of human finitude, which condemns the saint as well as the sinner to see ultimate reality 'through a glass darkly'. In order to think at all, the mind must take certain principles and definitions for granted. If then, as in philosophy, it turns upon these presuppositions to criticize them, it can do so only by using some criterion which is itself in need of further criticism. As it passes from point to point in its search for larger truth, the mind progresses mainly by noting resemblances between things that seem distinct from one another, and distinctions between things that resemble one another; but all such judgments require endless correction and restatement. Each word or concept that is redefined is relative to some other word or concept which itself needs to be clarified. And so we stick, to the end of our days, in the realm of partial and relative reality, to which our first childish explorations on the nursery floor introduced us.[1]

Once a man recognizes the limitations of human reason, and the impossibility of solving the riddle of the universe by science alone, or philosophy alone, or both together, he finds several alternatives open to him: he may try to be contented with the partial knowledge that he has, denying that anything more is either needful or possible; or, believing that something more is needful, he may despair of finding it, and therewith despair of life; or, he may seek a full solution along occultistic lines; or, mercifully, he may meet with a form of revelation which claims his central allegiance and sets him centrally at one with the Deepest Reality,

[1]Cf. Karl Heim, *Jesus der Herr*, pp. 18-31, where the finiteness of the human mind is described in terms of the principle of 'polarity'.

while leaving a multitude of secondary problems to be gradually worked out by the methods of science and philosophy. Whatever choice he makes involves more than a rational hypothesis; it involves a venture of faith, a hazard, into which his whole will is cast, and in which his whole destiny is at stake.

The first of these alternatives is that which was warmly defended by positivists and agnostics in the nineteenth century, and which has recently found able exponents in John Dewey (*A Common Faith*) and Julian Huxley (*Religion Without Revelation*). According to this school of thought, the religious quest for certainty is a wild goose chase, if it is carried out into the realm of 'ultimate' meanings and 'transcendental' realities; but there is scope enough for religious reverence and loyalty within the sphere of our ordinary human life, with its sacred social ties and its partial unity with supporting natural processes. Religious experiences like 'the feeling of forgiveness and grace to a soul struggling with the sense of sin, the poignant experience of the value of another's atonement, or of one's own suffering; the sense of communion with and peace in the realities that are around us',[1] are asserted to be real, *as experiences*; but it is argued that they can be adequately understood in purely secularistic terms, as natural responses to our

[1]Huxley, *op. cit.*, p. 317.

human associates and other realities that immediately and obviously surround and support us.

It would be wrong to deny genuine religious significance to 'the realities that are around us'. In all religions, something sacred has been seen in the family tie, in national solidarity, in the powers of nature that are immediately related to human needs; and in theistic religion, the power of God has been conceived to manifest itself in these sacred realities. But religious 'peace' is another matter. When a man tries to find religious peace through devoting himself to his family or throwing himself completely into some great political movement—as multitudes of people are trying to do in our time—he is surely destined for ultimate disillusionment, for he is attributing absolute significance to something which in itself possesses only relative significance. He is setting up an idol, which is sure in the end to be cast down. He is setting up a rival to the One True God, Who alone deserves man's whole hearted allegiance. If this One True God be a mere figment of the imagination, a vague and unsubstantiated hypothesis, as positivistic thinkers claim, He behaves in a highly realistic fashion—casting down the self-sufficient systems of civilization that attempt to do without Him, shattering the illusions that men wrap about their little substitute gods to conceal their inadequacy, tormenting men's souls until they turn to the Object which alone deserves their devotion, and which alone can give peace to their souls. An *Unknown* God He may be; but *unreal*—hardly! So long as this transcendent X in the cosmic equation remains unsolved, nothing is solved.

It is possible, of course, to interpret this situation in a radically sceptical and pessimistic sense. The thing which shatters our idols and our secular civilizations is perhaps not God, but a cruel and inscrutable Fate. There is *nothing* on which man may set his heart without being let down. 'Vanity of vanities, all is vanity!' There are some who have been led, like Tolstoy, to the verge of suicide by this feeling of the total meaninglessness of existence. Yet just on the brink of despair, where the sense of human helplessness reaches its climax, is the very spot where men experience a sudden access of hope, as Tolstoy did, and testify to their fellows that they have found God, or been found of Him. There are two main ways in which this miracle has been reported to have occurred: either by the overcoming of human limitations, so that we see through the veil of mystery by our own heightened powers; or by the breaking through of light and truth from the other side, so that divine reality comes to meet us where we live, and accommodates itself to our humble estate. The first way is the way of occultism; the second is the way of revelation.

It would be too easy to dismiss the various types of occultism on the hypothesis that they represent various forms of self-induced illusion. The religious seeker has reached the end of his rational tether, it might be said, and is delivered from his impasse only because the ideas over which he has been subconsciously brooding suddenly dart into his conscious mind with a weirdly convincing luminousness. There is much in the case, *e.g.*, of Emanuel Swedenborg to give colour to this hypothesis. But it is not necessary to take such a purely subjective view of occultistic phenomena, in order to recognize that they fail to satisfy our need of saving revelation. It is possible to believe that our ordinary human powers of cognition are truly heightened under certain conditions—that clairvoyance really occurs, that genuine communication with spiritual beings is possible, that great flashes of insight occur in mystical states, which penetrate deeply into certain dark recesses of this mysterious universe—and yet to note in all these extraordinary forms of knowledge that same imperfect, 'bit-by-bit' quality which gives to our other knowledge its characteristic mark of finitude. The psychic medium and the mystic may add to our common store of knowledge in their own way, as the scientist, the philosopher and the theologian may do in theirs; but if they fancy they have burst the bounds of finitude and unveiled *The Secret*, then they delude themselves and the multitudes who run after them. To study occult phenomena in a spirit of disinterested curiosity is to render a great service; to look for religious guidance in this sphere is to risk one's sanity and personal integrity.

There remains the possibility that God should condescend to our weakness, and reveal to us the secret of the meaning of life, which we cannot discover by ourselves. This is a very humiliating idea, acceptable only to the humble and contrite mind aware of its own limitations and reaching out in faith beyond them. It is an idea which has always been 'foolishness to the Greeks', and to all those who pride themselves upon the sufficiency of their intelligence; yet to whittle it down so as to eliminate all rational difficulties is almost surely to destroy it. It means *divine self-communication*, it means *divine initiative*, it means *divine self-giving*, or it means nothing. This is what we believe and teach, as Christians, so long as we remain Christian in the full sense of the word. This divine self-communication takes place in a *general* way, we believe, in the whole order of nature and the whole process of history; in a *special* way in the history of the 'chosen people' and its spiritual offspring, the Christian Church; in a *unique* way in Jesus Christ.

Emil Brunner is quite right when he maintains[1]

---

[1] Brunner, *The Mediator*, chap. i, 'The Distinction Between General and Special Revelation.'

that a theory of general revelation to which the Old and New Testament revelations are simply *added*, or of which they are regarded as *special instances*, can never be an adequate Christian theory. In general revelation, the divine initiative is hardly distinguishable from human discovery; and human misinterpretation of the message so garbles its meaning that, apart from further light, it gives us 'not half the truth but distorted truth'.[1] Nevertheless, there are certain attributes of God— the scope of His operations, the sweep of His purposes, the immensity of His power—which do not appear so well anywhere else, even in Christ, as they appear in this most general and impersonal form of the divine self-disclosure. In every place and time, men have bowed before the presence of a *mysterium tremendum*, something holy and august in the general structure and process of nature and history; and in the light cast backward by the Incarnation, this is seen to have been a first elementary act of self-disclosure, on the part of a God Who is for ever striving to communicate Himself to His creatures.

We come closer to the living centre of God's nature in His dealings with the 'chosen people'. There is nothing arbitrary, let it be said, in the 'choice'. A Will that seeks the good of all peoples must find a point of entrance into human affairs;

[1] *Ibid.* p. 33.

and suffering makes a people peculiarly sensitive to divine guidance. Many of us have experienced from time to time during the troublous years since 1914 a kind of emancipation from triviality, a sense of standing on the brink of eternity, that has enabled us to hear something in the Word of God which our ears were too dull to hear in times of peace and prosperity. Nothing, perhaps, but a like dullness of mind on their part had prevented God from speaking to other peoples the Word which He spoke to the Hebrew prophets; but be that as it may, the Word at any rate remained unspoken. It was to the Hebrews alone that God made Himself known as a living principle of Justice moving in the midst of human affairs, bringing down the proud, raising up the oppressed, preparing the way for the great Day of the Lord when all that is crooked shall be made straight, and the rough places even. The Hebrews alone, of all ancient peoples, never gave up their God in time of national disaster. They complained and lamented, and many fell away; but there was always a 'faithful remnant'; whereas all other conquered and oppressed peoples deserted their gods for the gods of their conquerors, the delusive gods of Power and Success. The true God, in Whose slowly grinding mills of justice all lesser deities must eventually be pulverized, was thus revealed only to His Suffering Servant, Israel.

As the special revelation of God's justice made
to the chosen people corrects and fulfils the general
revelation of His power in nature and history, so
the unique revelation of God's gracious, sacrificial
love made in Jesus Christ corrects and fulfils the
earlier revelation of His justice. It is to the revelation in Christ alone that Brunner's great word,
Einmaligkeit, 'once-for-all-ness', fully applies. The
Old Testament revelation is still general and
impersonal; it takes the form of law. If specific,
unrepeatable historic events help to make the
meaning of the divine Will behind the law more
concrete, no one of these events completely sums
up the series. God utters Himself in a succession
of mighty acts—great judgments and great deliverances—which run through the whole history
of Israel, and indeed cannot be thought to have
come to an end until the Jewish problem is finally
settled, and the Kingdom of God is come.[1] It is
the prophet's business to hear and interpret the
Word of God by brooding over the significance of
these events until he grasps and proclaims what
Karl Marx would call 'the dialectic of history'—
an essentially endless task, in which modern prophets have their *rôle* to play, as they brood over
the significance of God's acts in *these* momentous

[1]John MacMurray remarks in his *Creative Society* (p. 139)
that 'the solution of the Jewish problem and of the problem of
universal community is one and the same'.

times, and see modern history in the light of Old Testament prophecy. But in the Cross of Christ God's love is *once for all* revealed as His justice will not be revealed till the end of history; and in revealing to us His love, God puts us in touch with the centre of His being, His very heart and soul, which are elsewhere hidden by the general and impersonal working of the natural and moral orders. Jesus is not merely the prophetic interpreter of a divine act; He is Himself the act of God to be interpreted; and in this act God utters Himself so decisively that all other Words of God must be measured by this standard.[1] To call Him divine, measuring His divinity by the manifestation of God in nature or in Old Testament prophecy, is to judge the mountain by the foothills. There is no higher designation we can use than to call anything 'Christlike'. The forgiving love of God in Christ constitutes a species by itself, with only one typical instance.[2]

[1] The contrast which I have here in mind is expressed by Karl Heim in the form of a contrast between 'God's silent action', which the prophet must endeavour to interpret, and 'God's speech', which is uttered only in the life of Christ. (*Jesus der Herr*, pp. 177-187.) Both, of course, come under the conception of the Word in the Johannine sense.

[2] In emphasizing the 'once-for-allness' of the revelation of God in Christ, I have not meant to suggest that it is isolated, unrepeatable and so unverifiable. It is continually verified whenever a Christian finds peace with God through Christ ('Justification')

Walter M. Horton

The revelation of God in Christ casts a flood of light upon all previous and subsequent revelations. The vastness and impersonal regularity of God's working in nature—whether as glimpsed by the Psalmist or as more precisely set forth by modern astronomers—is seen to mean something other than the unconscious march of a mighty power indifferent to the fate of its creatures. The inexorability of God's moral judgments, which periodically and systematically destroy all social institutions that are not 'on the square', is seen to mean something more than a divine passion for law and order. 'Whom the Lord *loveth* he chasteneth.' There is love of course to be discerned in the God of Nature and the God of the Old Testament; yet we owe the clear vision of this fact, and the conviction of the ultimate unity of God's power and justice with His love, to the unique revelation given us in the life, death and victory of Christ.

It must not be supposed that with the coming of Christ all mysteries are at an end, all problems solved. On the contrary, the problems of metaphysics remain as difficult for the Christian philosopher as they were for Aristotle, and the enigma of the future has not yet been disclosed by the

and its meaning is continually reinterpreted as Christians in many specific positions in life seek guidance for daily conduct through the 'mind of Christ'. Moreover, it is confirmed by its power to unify and crown all other truth.

Sphinx, while a thousand practical difficulties still stand between us and the Kingdom which Christ said was 'at hand'. Man remains finite and God infinite, so that our human speculations about God continue to miscarry. But one thing is changed for ever, since Christ: We are no longer alone in the dark, grappling singlehanded with the powers of sin and death that assail us. We have the continuing companionship and guidance of One who makes plain to us, by His Spirit, as much of the Will of God as it is needful for us to know, and imparts to us by the same Spirit as much strength as we need to face the difficulties with which we are confronted. The chief question, 'What shall I do with my life?' is now answered; and the answer is, quite simply, 'Give yourself to Christ.' Give yourself, that is, to One who claims your supreme loyalty as no other leader can rightfully do, because He manifests to you an attitude of divine concern against which you have in the end no possible moral defence. Give yourself to One who empowers you to face life with that peace of mind which the world cannot give or take away, because He has overcome the world, having suffered the worst that ignorance and sin and death could do to Him, and risen victor over them all.

Since the Gospel of God's forgiving love in Christ thus stands supreme above all other divine revelations, and since divine revelation stands supreme above science and philosophy as an answer to the main problem of life, it is clear that Christian teaching is perverted when anything other than this Gospel is made central and normative. Other truth may be used to supplement and confirm the Gospel, to fill it out and correct it in matters of detail; but it cannot be used as a measuring rod to test the truth of the Gospel. That would be a reversal of values.

III. THE LIMITS OF REVELATION AND THE NEED OF 'NATURAL THEOLOGY'

If the revelation of God in Christ is so supremely important, the question arises whether anything more is needed; whether Christian teaching should not be drawn from this one source alone, and seek no other corroboration of the truth of its message than the testimony of the Holy Spirit. 'God is to be known only through God.' If men do not respond to the supreme revelation of God, when it is simply and unphilosophically presented to them, then, it may be urged, they will never respond to arguments based upon dimmer and more dubious forms of truth. To reason with sceptics about the truth of Christianity, using arguments drawn from nature and history, is to forget the dimness of the light of nature and the perversity of the human mind. Eventually, all 'natural theology' results in the acceptance of principles and axioms foreign to the Gospel, which impoverish and corrupt Christian teaching. Considerations of this sort are leading many contemporary Protestant thinkers, especially in Germany, under the threat of the 'new paganism', to revive the exclusivist slogans of the Reformation, and to assume a hostile attitude toward all attempts to rationalize the Gospel, or work out a Christian apologetic.

It is clear from the history of Christian thought that the Church never rests permanently content with any such irrationalism, nor is she likely to do so this time. In the heat of her conflict with resurgent paganism she may resolve, for the time being, to 'shoot only with weapons of the heaviest calibre' and so to confine herself strictly to the Gospel message; but in the long run she will not hesitate to employ the 'whole armour of God', which includes all truth. This is not primarily a question of strategy, but a question of reverence for truth. If it were merely a question of strategy, then one might admit the force of Karl Barth's contention, that the most successful apologetic is not one which is over-anxious to meet the rational objections of the sceptic, but one which simply and unapologetically expounds the Gospel.[1] But if God really reveals Himself in nature and history as well as in

[1]Karl Barth, *Nein! Antwort an Emil Brunner*, p. 62.

Christ, in law as well as in grace, in 'reason' as well as in 'revelation', these lesser lights cannot be spurned—however imperfect and insufficient they may be—without in some way falsifying or distorting the Gospel.

If it be argued that the revelation in Christ supersedes and fulfils all lesser lights, and includes all needful truth, this cannot be admitted in a sense that overlooks the peculiar nature of divine revelation. *Revelation, too, has its limitations.*[1] They are limitations of a very different character from the limitations of reason, but very real and not to be ignored without grave consequences. In the main, these limitations are the exact opposites of the limitations of science. Science is exact in matters of detail but extremely unbalanced in its total perspective. Revelation is fundamentally right in its total perspective but quite inexact in matters of detail. Science is bare and abstract. Revelation is concrete and full of rich meaning. But the meaning appears in its true significance only when revelation is used to interpret and cast light upon other truth. To rely upon revelation apart from other truth is as bad as to rely upon prayer apart from

[1]It is obvious that I mean *Revelation as humanly apprehended*, not *Revelation as divinely understood*. What we apprehend is never God Himself, in all the richness of His being, but something or someone that mediates the divine nature to us 'in a mystery', symbolically, and so needs endless clarification and interpretation.

action, or upon providence apart from intelligent forethought. Revelation is no substitute for reason; it is a fertile stimulus to fruitful understanding, as it is an inexhaustible source of inspiration for bold endeavour. If reason without revelation is blind, revelation without reason is a dazzling, unintelligible light. What Matthew Arnold said years ago about the *Homo unius libri* still holds good: the man who knows only scripture does not even know scripture. And we may add, the man who knows only Christ does not even know Christ.

There are some ancient misunderstandings about revelation which do not seriously threaten us at present, after the debates of the last half-century. We are not likely again to identify God's eternal Word with the Book which contains the record of its revealing, or to insist that everything in that Book is infallibly correct and verbally inspired. We are not likely to suppose that the authority of revelation extends into the sphere of fact and law, where natural science is supreme; nor are we likely, on the other hand, to attribute to scientific matters so great a religious significance as they appeared to have during the controversy over Darwinism. But in our new sense of the religious supremacy of Christian revelation, we are apt to disparage other forms of truth, and so in the long run undermine faith in revelation itself, since the faith which accepts it will seem to be a blind faith. Because revelation is a gift from on high, which human science and invention could never have produced, we are apt to underestimate the importance of the human side in the process of revelation, the condition of aspiration and receptivity which makes the transmission of the divine light possible.

Let it be granted at once that man is finally dependent upon divine light and grace, and has nothing that he has not received. Neither revelation nor redemption is adequately describable in terms of 'synergism'. The 'delegated spontaneity' whereby man 'cooperates' in his own enlightenment and salvation is like all his powers ultimately derived from God. His dependence upon God is as absolute as St. Augustine insisted it was. Yet St. Augustine himself, when describing his own gradual approach to an acceptance of Christian revelation, lays great stress upon that *love of truth* which was awakened in him, years before his conversion, by the reading of Cicero's *Hortensius*. Without this previous enlightenment, which he rightly attributes to the guidance of God working through this pagan author, the saint would never have been ready to receive the Gospel; nor can any man receive it who has not within himself some inner principle of light, to testify to its truth. Say if you will that the 'natural man' has no inner light to guide him, because he is a fallen creature; but then the 'natural man' becomes a pure abstraction, an artificial residuum which remains when the presence of God's grace and power have been completely thought away from human life.

That man exists at all—or as Brunner would put it, his mere 'formal' essence as a responsible self—is evidence that he embodies enough of the grace of God to make him capable of response to the Gospel. But it is doubtful whether in any given case the divine light that is present with a man is reducible to this absolute formal minimum. In a 'material' as well as in a 'formal' sense, the grace of God and the light of God are playing all about us, and reaching us through many humble and unsuspected channels, so that they become a part of our nature by a process of unconscious assimilation. Hence is that power to know a better way, even while following the worse, to which St. Paul bears witness. Unless this inward presence of the Spirit of God in the soul of man is admitted, and recognized as a necessary preparation for the acceptance of the Gospel, the giving of faith to some and not to others becomes once more a matter of arbitrary divine choice, and double pre-destination is already implied—in which case, it becomes our sacred duty to detest and reject the celestial tyrant so described, and refuse to recognize Him as God! No man of course can *deserve*

the presence of the Spirit of God more than another man; but to some men it comes more fully
than to others, by virtue of the circumstances of
their upbringing; and these fortunate ones have
it as their great responsibility to open up channels
of divine light and grace for the less fortunate.
The Word of God is meant for all; but only those
who are inwardly prepared, through channels
which are at least partly human and comprehensible, are able to receive it.

If all receiving of truth, even in its humblest
forms—'reason' as well as 'revelation'—is the receiving of divine self-impartation, and may open
the way to the receiving of the full truth of the
Gospel, then all truth is in some sense germane to
theology. The ideal of a theology that shall be
veritably 'Queen of the Sciences' seems more remote to us today than to the mediaeval mind,
partly because of the vast increase in the bulk of
secular science, and partly because of our increased
sense of the radical diversities and limitations of
the various fields of knowledge. That all truth
constitutes one 'system of God', from the divine
point of view, is a postulate without which Christian thought tends toward fanaticism and obscurantism; but the difficulty of correctly visualiz-
ing this final harmony is such as to discourage the
attempt to be too completely rational and systematic in one's thinking. While our human appre-

hension of divine truth remains fragmentary, it is well to maintain a number of departments of theological investigation, relatively independent of one another, so as to act as checks and balances against each other's errors. One of these departments is known as biblical theology. Another is known as natural theology. The former is more important than the latter, for Christian teaching, because it enables us to distinguish the substance of 'special' and 'unique' revelation from the 'earthen vessel' in which it has come down to us; but neither biblical nor natural theology can stand alone, and each needs the correction of the other.

Natural theology—today the object of such severe attack on the part of the champions of the Reformation doctrine of *scriptura sola*—may be variously defined, and seems to be variously conceived by its opponents. Let us discriminate two senses of the term, at least. By 'natural theology' may be meant, in the first place, what the name literally implies: a doctrine of God directly inferred from the phenomena of nature, as they appear to the secular mind, without reference to religious faith and experience; a strictly and purely 'rational' theology. Plato and Aristotle in ancient times, Newton and Paley in the eighteenth century, cultivated natural theology in this sense. Francis Bacon defined it succinctly as 'Divine

Philosophy . . . that spark of the knowledge of God which may be had by the light of nature and the consideration of created things . . . divine in respect of its object, and *natural* in respect of its source of information'.[1] In a second and wider sense, 'natural theology' may be understood as equivalent to philosophy of religion: that branch of religious thought in which the testimony of all religions is given a hearing, and in the light of this testimony certain basic affirmations are made, not as matters of *faith*, but as inductions from general experience, including religious experience ('reason' plus 'general revelation'). D. C. Macintosh's *Theology as an Empirical Science*, H. N. Wieman's *Wrestle of Religion with Truth*, and the symposium on *Religious Realism* to which they and other American theologians recently (1931) contributed, are to be described in this second sense as a kind of natural theology. In both senses, natural theology has a real though strictly limited contribution to make to Christian thought.

In the narrower and more precise sense, natural theology has as its main task the exploration of the theistic implications of the natural sciences. It should be quite clear by now that the concept of God which emerges from such a survey is not only sub-Christian but sub-religious; yet if nature is a

[1] *De Augm.*, iii. 2. Cf. C. C. J. Webb, *Studies in the History of Natural Theology*, p. 2, and *passim*.

sphere of the divine operation, as the Bible itself affirms, then all the natural sciences cast light upon the natural attributes of God, and contribute to general revelation. There is a continuing need for scientific theologians like Bishop Barnes or Professor Tennant to specialize in this field, and keep Christian thought in touch with significant scientific developments. Unless man is so preposterously powerful as to be able to infect the whole fair framework of nature with his corruption, the order of creation still is 'very good' and declares the glory of God. If science, with its careful impersonality and exact measurement, does not declare significant truth about this order, then all thought is delusion and all belief a mad gamble.

In the wider sense, as philosophy of religion, natural theology has a still more important contribution to make. It cannot hope, of course, to turn the whole Christian faith into a system of theosophical gnosis, confirmed by science, philosophy, and the convergent testimony of all religions. When it attempts so much—as Hegel's *Philosophy of Religion* did in effect—it caricatures the Christian faith, and renders itself ridiculous. But if the Incarnate Word is one with 'the light that lighteth every man that cometh into the world', as the Gospel of John affirms, then some aspects at least of Christian revelation are capable of confirmation through their congruity with various non-Chris-

tian lines of general revelation, and through their
congruity with common rational knowledge. Religious truth is so precious that to raise any portion
of it, however small, from the rank of vague conjecture to that of verified knowledge is a matter of
cardinal importance. Particularly in our time,
when so many are convinced that the idea of God
is a mere subjective delusion, it is valuable to
establish it as a matter of knowledge that *some*
divine reality, whatever its ultimate nature may be,
is surely *there*. If the top of the mountain of God is
for ever beyond our ken, its base is in our midst,
and should be susceptible of investigation if the
mountain is really there at all. The method of investigation is rational, and roughly analogous to
that by which all human *knowledge*, as distinct
from vague intuition, is gained: comparison of
experiences of men in many times and places, for-
mulation of a general concept to cover all these
data, logical elaboration of this concept, and its
testing by further observation and experience. It
is by this method that the American 'religious
realists' claim God is knowable—although they
recognize that what is knowable is never the whole
truth about God. Their trust in reason (now understood as *reason enriched by the data of religious experience*) is parallel to that of the Roman Church,
which affirms that reason can establish *that* God is,
although it needs the further light of revelation to

know adequately *what* He is. They differ from traditional Thomism in that they stress the cosmological and teleological arguments less heavily than the argument from moral and religious experience.

Christian dogmatics, or systematic theology, can never be content with the results of natural theology in *either* of the above senses; but it cannot subscribe to any definition of its task and method which condemns it to irrationality.[1] Its primary datum is the unique revelation of God in Jesus Christ, and its secondary datum is the special revelation of God in that sacred history which began with the rise of Hebrew prophecy and is still continued through the interaction of the synagogue and the church with their modern secular environment. To these data, Christian theology must be faithful, or it will lose its *raison d'être*. But it must use rational methods in ex-

[1]The contrast here made between natural theology and dogmatics is parallel to the contrast between 'The God of Human Experience' and 'The God of Christian Faith' in my *Theism and the Modern Mood*. The only difference is that since writing *Theism and the Modern Mood* I have come to stress the objective side of revelation (divine self-disclosure) more than the subjective attitude of *venturesome faith* which is its human correlative and condition. Unless men dare to reach out in faith, God does not reveal Himself to them; but when He does reveal Himself, His faithful servants never claim to have found Him by their daring, but rather to have *been* found by His patient, outgoing mercy, which somehow managed to unlock the door from the inside, and so let itself in.

pounding and confirming the super-rational revelation committed to its care, unless it is willing to assume that God is irrational, and His world radically chaotic; and it must integrate revelation with common knowledge as far as possible. It must affirm that when reason is enlightened by religious insight ('general' revelation) and inspired by Christian faith ('special' and 'unique' revelation) it surpasses itself, and adumbrates a *Weltanschauung* that bestows infinite richness of meaning upon each least event. It is an incomplete *Weltanschauung*, necessarily, for Christian revelation points forward to a 'new heaven and a new earth', of which we have only hints and tokens in this present world order. Theology can never be experimental in the same sense as science, since the experiments of religion cannot be completed under control conditions, in a brief span of space-time. They are more like the experiments of politics, which take centuries to perform, and require steadfast faith in a goal that remains invisible. Theology is inevitably *Glaubenslehre*, 'faith-doctrine'. But the faith to which it is loyal is not a blind faith. It is kindled by a revelation which is itself luminous; which awakens our ambition to fit all known truth together according to the pattern given us in Christ, and to face the hosts of darkness fearlessly in His name, while waiting for the 'scattering of all shadows'.

By the Right Rev. Dr. GUSTAF AULÉN

Bishop of Strängnäs, Sweden

Some twenty years ago one of our best Swedish theologians, who had himself done very much for a theological revival in Sweden, told me that he preferred to avoid the words 'religion' and 'revelation', when speaking about Christian faith and life. He thought those words to be dangerous and more adapted to conceal than to reveal what Christianity really means. And certainly the way in which they have been used in the history of Christian thought has not always been commendable. The word 'religion' is heavily burdened with relativism. If you would begin with a statement about religion that is supposed to express what is common to all religions, you have placed Christianity in a connexion where its true essence never will be found. The word 'revelation' is heavily burdened with intellectualism. Theology has often combined Reason and Revelation as two ways towards the knowledge of God. If you would try to say what revelation may add to the knowledge of God reached through reason, you would be speaking of another God than the God of Christian faith. Certainly the Christian faith is conscious of having a true knowledge of God. But this knowledge does not mean only certain ideas or a certain doctrine about a being called God; it means a personal relation brought into existence through the action of God. And therefore, if we are to use the word revelation in our Christian language, revelation must always be connected with *the activity of God*; it must signify the self-communication of God through His own activity. This self-communication of God is, in the language of faith, known as 'revelation'. Revelation therefore does not mean only that I have obtained some knowledge of God in the same manner as I may obtain other knowledge about nature and humanity; it means that God Himself has acted for my enlightenment through Him who is Himself 'the Word of God', in this way unveiling to me His heart.

I. THE PRESENT SITUATION

It will be best to begin with a positive statement of the Christian understanding of revelation. Nothing could in fact be more important in the present situation than to give such a statement in clear and plain words. Probably some among us would rather fix their hopes on apologetical endeavours on psychological or philosophical lines. I will not deny that such endeavours can be helpful. But two things seem to me obvious. If you would defend anything, the first condition is to know what it is that you are defending; and no apology for Christian faith will be of any use without a clear conception of the Christian message. Secondly: the best and at bottom the only effective apology is the Christian message itself. In proportion as the Christian message is explained in all its own strength and majesty, simplicity and richness, theology has performed its most important and primary task.[1]

Surveying the theological situation as it has developed in the last two decades, I venture to say that its most characteristic note has been theology's growing consciousness of its own nature. It

[1]Certainly it is also an important task of theology that it should give an analysis and exhibition of the grounds of the faith. Much might be said about this question. And much has been said about it in the other papers in this book. Yet in the end even this analysis must fall back upon the fact of revelation, in so far as revelation is the ultimate ground of faith. The ultimate ground of any faith is always the fact that I have been conquered by the voice of the revealed God. When that happens to me I cannot but say, 'Here God truly speaks, and there is no other God but He.' The last word as regards the ground of my Christian faith remains the old biblical word: 'Other foundation can no man lay than that is laid, which is Jesus Christ.'

has found it necessary to enter deeper and deeper into the question of the real nature of Christianity. The situation was indeed dangerous. There was a great risk that Christianity would lose its soul. Since the time of the Enlightenment Christianity had in many different ways been combined and confused with a religiosity of a humanistic and idealistic kind, which was more a glorification of man than a glorification of God. This religiosity had a considerable influence especially amongst educated people. The dominant theology had largely failed to resist this influence; it had on the contrary cooperated with the dominant intellectual forces and had so itself prepared the way for the new religious syncretism. In this work theology was guided by the best intentions; the aim was to present an apologia for Christianity and to open doors for it in the modern intellectual world. Nevertheless the result was disastrous. The Christian message was changed, transformed and weakened, and its power was stolen through an alliance with an alien religious spirit.

It was indeed high time that the properly Christian self-consciousness should be revived in the theological world. It was high time that theology should turn again and resist the influences that had obscured the Christian message and concealed what Christianity really means.

Theology has had to fight a similar battle at

several different periods in the history of Christendom. Christianity has indeed always to fight for its existence: for there is always opposition to overcome. The Christian confession of faith cannot be preserved like capital in a bank; it can only be preserved by being perpetually learnt afresh. Nevertheless there have been special times of crisis when the conflict for the Christian message has been more acute than at other times. I will here recall three of the main earlier occasions.

Christianity was born in conflict and has grown up in conflict. The gospels show us on every page the opposition that existed between Jesus and the spiritual leaders of the Jewish people, and how this opposition led to the Cross. Then Christianity came into existence with the confession of faith in the Resurrection, in the living *Kyrios*. The work of Jesus had not been in vain; He really was 'He that should come'. He had won the victory. This confession of faith in the Resurrection separated the young Christianity from the Jewish religion and was at the same time the expression of its own self-consciousness.

The first great crisis in the history of Christendom came in the time of the ancient Church. This crisis was essentially a conflict between Christianity and Hellenistic mystery religion of various kinds; there was a great danger lest Christianity should disappear in a syncretistic religiosity. But it was saved through the ancient Church's confession of faith in Christ, the confession which has its centre in the Incarnation, because it is God Himself who in and through Christ has accomplished the work of salvation.

The second great crisis belongs to the time of the Reformation. Here again we have a conflict against a religious syncretism, against a confusion of Christianity with foreign elements that threatened to obscure the Christian message of salvation through God's love in Christ alone. Since the confession by the Reformers of 'Justification by Faith' means a confession of salvation through the love of God in Christ alone, it is therefore a confession of the universal Christian faith and a new expression of the Christian self-consciousness.

It is right to consider the present situation in the light of these earlier crises in the history of Christendom. In this light we understand better our own position as well as the task that lies before Christian thought in our day. It is obvious that there lies behind us—if we can dare to say 'behind' —a third period characterized by religious syncretism. The risk has obviously been that Christianity should be weakened and diluted into a vague idealistic religiosity, which in fact transforms Christianity into a religious embellishment of human life and makes this religiosity a substitute for real Christianity. The conditions of human life are idealized, and therefore the great Christian words, even if they are still used, lose their real original and proper sense. It is still possible to speak of sin; but 'sin' is made to mean something that belongs only to the 'lower' nature of man, not to his 'higher', 'divine' and 'immortal' nature. The nature of man here is divided into two parts, and man is no longer regarded as a whole, as a totality; hence sin is not, as it is for the Christian faith, the selfishness that belongs just to the soul, to the 'heart' of man. So again, while it is still possible to speak of 'salvation', 'salvation' is not regarded as a salvation of man as a whole, but only as a strengthening of the 'divine' part of man. The significance of Christ is then that He represents the highest ideal of humanity. The Kingdom of God is considered from an immanent and evolutionary point of view: the thought is that the kingdom more and more reaches its perfection within the limits of human history.

It ought to be observed that this view often tried to seek support from biblical investigations. It was said to correspond to 'the religion of Jesus' as opposed to apostolic Christianity. In reality, however, this supposed opposition between Jesus and the apostles existed only in the imagination of the theologians. The fact was that the theologians interpreted the texts of the gospels in the light of their own 'modern' ideas, and so confused the message of Jesus with their own humanistic religiosity.

When we consider the situation during the last two centuries, it is impossible to deny that Christianity has been living in a period of religious syncretism. In such a situation nothing can be more necessary than for Christianity to reassert its own nature in self-defence. But before saying what such a self-defence can mean, I ought perhaps to say what it does not mean. The self-defence of Christianity has sometimes been confused with a purism that would isolate the Christian message from the human life around it. Such an attitude would be a fatal misunderstanding. It is certainly necessary for Christian thought to live the life of its own day in communication with the world around; we must fully admit that thoughts as well as rituals, that have grown up in another soil than the Christian, *can* be baptized into Christ. But on the other hand Christianity must never compromise with a religiosity that attacks the very heart of Christian faith. The real self-defence of Christianity is a conflict against a religiosity which from the Christian point of view must be condemned as false.

The opposition to Christianity can act in different ways. It can meet Christianity in open conflict. But it can also enter into negotiations with Christianity and try to make terms with it.

That is far more dangerous, because in a confusion of ideas the powers of the Christian faith are easily stolen away. Wherever a confusion of this kind appears, it is for Christianity a matter of life or death not to surrender but to strengthen its own self-consciousness.

If now we look back to the great crises in the history of Christendom, it is evident that every crisis has its own character; nevertheless it would not be wrong to say that at bottom the opposition has always been one and the same. It is the same opposition returning in a different dress. The opposition may appear as Jewish moralism or as Hellenistic mysticism or as modern humanistic religiosity—the heart of the opposition is always the same. The great enemy of Christianity has from the beginning till today been *the religiosity of man's self-glorification*. The essence of the opposition has always consisted in the worship of created things instead of the Creator.

The events of the last years have, in fact, made the situation far clearer than it was before. They have snatched away the veils that concealed the naked truth. We live in difficult times, full of unrest in all departments of life. As regards Christianity, there has arisen a hostility to it, organized as it has never been since the first Christian centuries. New religious corporations have been organized, which confess themselves to be non-Christian. We have all heard much about the 'new heathenism' in Germany. The appearance of this 'German faith movement' is very instructive. It has not appeared suddenly. It is as evident as possible that this movement has its roots in the previous age; it is a child of the humanistic religiosity that during the last centuries has been confused with Christianity. The difference is only that now the Christian elements have been rejected and expelled, and that the attitude has become more collectivistic than individualistic. If in the religious syncretism of the last centuries the Christian elements more or less concealed the inherent element of human self-glorification, this self-glorification now appears in all its nakedness, primarily as a glorification of 'the race and the blood'. At the same time we see here with terrifying clearness that a humanistic religiosity left to itself cannot save humanity—because it denies the Love that does not seek its own and that transcends all human limits.

II. INCARNATION

What does the Christian faith say about the revelation of God? All that it says centres in the focus of the Incarnation. Its first and its last word is that God is incarnate in Christ and that through Him we get to know the heart of God.

The confession of faith in the Incarnation was formulated in the ancient Church. But it was no invention of the Church. 'The Word was made flesh, and dwelt among us, and we beheld his glory, glory as of the only begotten of the Father, full of grace and truth.' These words in the first chapter of the Gospel of St. John speak of the Incarnation in more definite words than we find elsewhere in the New Testament. But the theme itself we find everywhere in the New Testament.

The confession of faith in the Incarnate does not mean that the Christian faith would deny all revelation of God outside Christ. The Epistle to the Hebrews says that God in many forms and fashions has spoken of old to our fathers by the prophets. St. Paul says in the Epistle to the Romans that the invisible nature of God has been perceptible in the things that He has made. The Christian view is at once universal and exclusive. It does not determine any limit for the revelation of God; but it knows no other God than the God Who reveals His heart in the life and work of Christ, and it insists that no one knows the Father except the Son and he to whom the Son reveals Him. The consequence of this double-sidedness is that all that claims to be a revelation of God must be examined and required to vindicate itself in the presence of God's revelation in Christ.

Gustaf Aulén

In the history of Christian thought we can often observe this tension between the universality and the exclusiveness of the Christian view. Such a tension can also be found in the missionary work of the Christian Church. It is, in fact, inseparable from the life of Christian faith. It cannot be removed through the compromises which a scholastic or an idealistic theology has tried to make. A compromise is possible only if the question of revelation be considered as a question of quantity. It is, however, not quantity but quality that separates the revelation of God in Christ from all that otherwise is called revelation. The decisive thing is that a new relation between God and man has been created through the work of God in Christ. It is because of this new relation that no one knows the Father except he to whom the Son reveals Him.

Christian theology speaks of a 'general' revelation in nature and history. And certainly the Christian faith finds a revelation of God in nature as well as in history. Nevertheless, there are great risks connected with the idea of a 'general' revelation. Instead of the principle that all that claims to be a revelation must be examined and vindicated in the light of Christ, the 'general' revelation has sometimes been put on the same level as the revelation of God in Christ, and the latter then considered only as a complement of the former.

Sometimes, indeed, the superiority even has been ascribed to the 'general' revelation.

When Christian faith finds a revelation of God in nature, this attitude goes back to the Old Testament: 'The heavens declare the glory of God, and the firmament sheweth His handy-work' (Psalm xix); and this note has never ceased to sound in Christianity. But while the Christian faith rightly speaks about the revelation of the majesty of God in nature, two things ought to be observed. In the first place, this 'natural theology' would be misused, if it were understood as a matter of rationality and not of faith. Thus, for instance, to find something of God revealed in nature is not to start from an idea of the world's suitability for its purpose, and from this starting point to reach conclusions about the providence of God. Even if it were possible in this way to demonstrate the providence of a God, this 'God' would have in common with the God of the Christian faith nothing but the name. Further, it must be said that such a thesis is far from self-evident. We find in the world of nature very much that gives us an impression of an absence of providence, of something meaningless, cold and insensible, and that is more a difficulty than a help to faith in God. Secondly: even though the Christian faith does speak of a revelation of God in nature, this revelation in itself appears as imperfect and fragmentary: it does not reveal the heart of God. I will here quote two verses from a Swedish hymn as typical of the outlook of faith:

> *True, nature glorious and rich*
> *With thousand voices' sound*
> *Has said to my fainthearted thought*
> *That Thou art great, O God.*
>
> *But yet Thy meaning was concealed,*
> *Thy heart I did not find.*
> *And in a dark and endless space*
> *I vanished like the dust.*

When we come from nature to history the situation is still more complicated. True, in history faith has heard the voice of God through the voices of men; in history it has seen God incarnate and found His heart. But if history, therefore, in a higher way than nature, is the place of the revelation of God, that does not apply to history as a whole. Every attempt to find in history as a whole a reflection of the will of God, or to read God's will in the events of history as in an open book, must fail. It is not only God's will that is to be found in history. There is also another will to be found there, which is more opposed to the will of God than the brightest brightness is to the darkest darkness. History is a drama, the arena of a conflict between the will of God and this opposed will. The Christian believes that the rule is in God's hand. But this rule cannot be demonstrated. History is a book full of riddles and sealed with seals that we cannot open.

When it speaks of a 'general' revelation, Christian theology has also combined its faith in the Creator with the thought of a revelation of God in man, since man has been created in the image of God. This revelation has sometimes been called the original revelation. Here we touch a point where the thoughts of theology have perhaps been more confused than elsewhere. It is here specially important to distinguish between ideas that really belong to the Christian faith and ideas that lead to a deification of man and therefore belong to a religiosity which is opposed to the Christian faith. 'The image of God' is supposed to stand for a divine element in man, and much endeavour has been spent to show that this divine part of man has not been destroyed by sin. Where this thought dominates, there is no difference between 'the highest human' and 'the divine'. The faith in the Creator, which aims at the glorification of God, has here been used rather to serve the self-glorification of man. Sometimes also this theory about the divine element in man has been used for the purpose of giving a rational explanation of the possibilities of salvation. It need scarcely be said that such explanations do not correspond with faith's own view as to the saving Love of God.

When faith speaks about an original revelation given to man at the creation, that does not mean that we should follow the way of mysticism and seek 'in the depths of our souls' to find something 'divine'; it means primarily two things. It means that God the Creator has a claim on us and that the destiny and purpose of man, given to him by God, is that he should be a member of the Kingdom of God. This view of the position of man as created by God includes the responsibility of man.

Two dangers, then, threaten theology in the questions that we have now touched: one is the isolation of the revelation of God in Christ; another is the use of the 'general' revelation in a way that leads to a deification of man or of human ordinances. In the theology of today we find both those lines of thought represented. In view of the period of religious syncretism in which we have been living, the isolating tendency can be easily accounted for as a reaction. On the other hand, it is obvious that, for instance in the present German theology, we meet a very dangerous teaching as to the divine character of what is called 'the ordinances of creation'. There are theologians who begin with clear and true words about the 'ordinances', in, or under, which God has set us to work, about the Christian's duty towards his neighbour, his family, his nation, his State—and who end with something like a deification of the

State. It must be allowed that the 'ordinances' in, and under, which we live, are gifts of God; but it is a long way from this starting point to the conclusion that the State *as it is* ought to be considered as a divine power—such a statement cannot be made without ignoring the sinful and daemonic powers that are at work in human life, and it will lead us away from the Christian principle that we must obey God rather than man.

This question of the relation between the revelation of God in Christ and revelation elsewhere contains one further problem—that of the relation between the Old and the New Testament. This question has never ceased to occupy Christian thought, and recently it has gained a new actuality. I am not thinking so much of the anti-Semitic movements of our day, and the claim that Christianity ought to be 'purified' from all Jewish elements, not only from the Old Testament but also from the Jewish elements in the New Testament and especially from St. Paul, and that Christianity then ought to appear as an Aryan 'heroism'. I am rather thinking of serious theological discussion. Harnack proposed, as is well known, that the Old Testament should be omitted from the canon of the Christian Church. He was following a line in Protestant theology that goes back to Schleiermacher. Neither of them understood what its continuity with the Old

Testament means for Christianity. On the other hand, there are today theologians who declare that the Old and the New Testament contain simply the same revelation: God reveals Himself to us 'in the same image' as He did under the old dispensation. The same only begotten Son, who is the Father's image for us, was also revealed to Israel.

Neither of these points of view can be vindicated as a genuine expression of the Christian faith. The first neglects the actual continuity of revelation in which Christ stands, and the second, very much against its own will, obscures the fundamental importance of the Incarnation. It is necessary to emphasize equally strongly the continuity of revelation and the fact that a new Covenant was founded through Christ. Christ is at once the fulfiller of the old revelation and the end of the old Covenant. Christ stands in an indissoluble continuity with the Old Testament. His God is the God of the patriarchs and the prophets. But at the same time the old is gone and the new has come. 'The new' is chiefly seen in His work, in His victory over the powers of evil, in the new Covenant that He brings and through which a new age has begun. It lies in the fulfilment of the work of salvation that God Himself accomplishes through Christ. But this fulfilment means at the same time a new revelation of God which unveils the depths of His love.

Through this revelation Christ is at the same time the fulfilment and the transformer of the revelation of the old Covenant. I cannot here give a full investigation of the questions that belong to this subject, and that have been much discussed in recent times. I must confine myself to a few short statements. The God who reveals Himself in the life and work of Christ is the Holy God of the old Covenant. His claims on man have not diminished but increased. His severity is not weakened but intensified. But at the same time His love has been revealed in a way that transcends all earlier revelations. Two features ought especially to be emphasized. The first is that the love of God comes to seek and save that which is sinful and unworthy. Certainly even the old Covenant had spoken much about the love and the mercy of God. But this love was there more or less confined to those who walked the way of righteousness, or at least to those who were standing in the Covenant and who through this position had got some worthiness and dignity. The love of God had not the character of spontaneous love and free grace towards men who have no worthiness of any kind. The second feature is that the incarnate love of God in Christ goes the way of sacrifice unto death.

The Old Testament has three main words: law, prophecy and sacrifice. As regards all three we

see the same combination of fulfilment and transformation that we have just observed. The law is
fulfilled in the commandment in which all com-
mandments are concentrated, the commandment
of a love that is like the love of the Father in
Heaven, and at the same time Christ is the end
of the law, since God's spontaneous, sacrificial
and victorious love in Christ addresses itself to
sinful and unworthy man. The way to God is no
more the way of the law, but the way of God's
love to man. Prophecy is fulfilled, but it is at the
same time transformed, since the Kingdom of
God is a universal kingdom and a kingdom that
does not belong to this world. Sacrifice is fulfilled
in the perfect sacrifice of Christ, but it is at the
same time transformed, since the sacrifice is now
not only a sacrifice offered to God—as it was in
Israel and in all the religions of the world—but
also a sacrifice in which the love of God itself
makes the sacrifice.

III. RESURRECTION

When we are considering what revelation means
for the Christian faith, the Resurrection calls
urgently for our attention. There are deep reasons
for this. Firstly, we must observe that Christianity
was born with the faith in the Resurrection and
that the Resurrection is the focus in which the

whole original Christian faith centres. The Christian Church is the child of the Resurrection. Its first task was to testify that Jesus was in truth 'He that should come', the Messiah and the *Kyrios*. Without the Resurrection, Jesus would have been for the disciples a false messiah. But the faith in the Resurrection was not only the power that started the Christian mission and gave it its confidence. It was also the decisive content of the Christian message. All that the original Christianity preaches is immediately connected with the Resurrection and gets its characteristic colour through this connexion. If one were to eliminate the Resurrection and retain only the other elements of the Christian message in the New Testament, the result would be that one would preserve only disconnected and disparate elements which then, in fact, would lose their original meaning; the power that creates unity and coherence between them would have disappeared.

All the Christian subjects of faith—the idea of God, Christology, salvation, the Kingdom of God, the Church, the sacraments, eschatology, etc.— get their characteristic colour through faith in the Resurrection. But I must confine myself to some words about salvation and the Kingdom of God.

It has already been said that the Christian faith sees the revelation of God from the point of view

of activity. This point of view is strongly emphasized through the faith in the Resurrection. The
Resurrection says that the revelation of God in
Christ is a conflict against the powers of evil and
that this conflict ended in victory. According to
the Gospels Jesus Himself saw His work as such
a conflict. He had been sent to fight the daemonic
powers that are opposed to the will of God. 'If it
is by the finger of God that I cast out demons, then
the reign of God has reached you already.' It is not
possible to understand the New Testament idea
of salvation apart from its dualistic background.
The dualism that we find here is not a metaphysical dualism between the infinite and the
finite, nor is it an absolute dualism as in the
Manichean teaching where Evil is an eternal
principle; it is religious dualism between the will
of God and that which in His created world resists
His will. The conflict of Jesus with the powers of
evil leads to His sacrifice and to His apparent
defeat on the Cross, but the apparent defeat was
in fact a victory and this victory was attested by
the Resurrection.

It is obvious that the original Christian faith in
the New Testament sees the life and work and
death of Jesus in the light that proceeds from the
Resurrection. The Cross is immediately and
inseparably connected with the Resurrection, and
draws therefrom its significance as the Cross of

salvation. The Cross does not stand as an isolated fact. The theory of the Atonement which later in history was formulated by St. Anselm, is seen from this point of view to be a transformation of the idea of the New Testament. A clear sign of the change of idea is the fact that the Resurrection has for his theory only a secondary importance. This supplanting of the Resurrection means undoubtedly a thoroughgoing transformation of the earlier view concerning God's work of salvation in and through Christ. For the original Christian view of the Resurrection cannot be thus put aside. It stands as inseparably connected with the sacrifice; it reveals Christ as Victor over the destroying powers of sin and death. It is at the same time communion with God through forgiveness, and life from the life of God. Victory over these destroying powers is the primary and essential content of the work of salvation that God performs in and through Christ. When this work of salvation is considered from the point of view of sacrifice, it is seen to be at the same time a work of atonement. The sacrifice is then not only a sacrifice on behalf of mankind, but at the same time and in the first place, a sacrifice made by the love of God. 'God was in Christ, reconciling the world unto himself.' The original Christian confession of faith in the Resurrection is first of all a confession of victory. 'Thanks be to God, which giveth us the victory through our Lord Jesus Christ.'

The Resurrection is, for the Christian faith, the decisive act of God between the Creation and the last Judgment. It is in this light that Christian faith regards the Kingdom of God. A new 'age' has come. The Christians live in a time of waiting. The Resurrection tells us that the kingdom has been founded and that it is on the way, but at the same time that it does not belong to this world. Two views of the Kingdom of God must be rejected. Firstly, the evolutionary view, the thought that the Kingdom of God will be perfectly realized in the life of history. The Christian faith cannot accept this idea as true. It knows that the Kingdom has an eschatological character, and that it never will be fulfilled in this world. Secondly, that idea of the Kingdom must also be rejected which speaks of the eschatological character of the Kingdom in metaphysical categories, and therefore separates the Kingdom and the world of history by an unbridgeable gulf. The Christian faith knows that the powers of the Kingdom are at work here and now; it knows, above all, that the living Lord Himself fights the battle of the Kingdom in the world of human life, and that in this continued conflict He is, through His Spirit, realizing the victory that He has once won. As Luther says: 'He strikes and strangles incessantly the enemies against whom He once wrestled.' In this fight of the Kingdom there are defeats as well as victories. The Christian believes with all his heart that power and majesty belong to the love of God. But he cannot deny that in this world God's love often seems to be a lost love.

Standing as he does in the time of waiting, in the aeon or 'age' between the Resurrection and the last Judgment, the Christian belongs to two worlds, to the world in which he lives and to the world that is the object of his hope. The Communion of Christ in the aeon between the Resurrection and the last Judgment is the Church, which is created and maintained through Christ and His Spirit, which is the Holy Spirit of God. To be a Christian means to be a member of the Church of Christ. There is no such thing as an 'individualistic' Christianity. Certainly the voice of God speaks to the individual soul. But that does not mean that the Christian should stand alone. His life as a Christian is a life of fellowship (κοινωνία) *in* the community and *for* the community. 'The Church is the Mother, that gives life to and that nourishes every Christian' (Luther). The Christian has his membership in the Church through the grace of God, received in faith. Since faith is born by the love of God in Christ and His Spirit working here and now in the Church, by means of the Word and sacraments, faith means communion with God here and now. But faith means at the same time hope—hope to look for the Resurrection of the dead and the life of the world to come. To lay stress upon faith as communion is not to weaken the importance of faith as hope. On the contrary, the more faith is communion with God and with the living Christ, who sitteth on the right hand of the Father, the more it is also a living hope.

IV. FORGIVENESS OF SINS ('JUSTIFICATION') AND THE NEW LIFE

When writing about revelation it is necessary to say some words about the personal relationship to God constituted by the revelation of God in Christ.

The revelation of God is fulfilled in Christ, but it is at the same time continually going on. The work of Christ is once for all finished through His sacrifice and His victory, but it is at the same time a continuing work of the living Lord. The forgiveness of sins is the permanent work of Christ, through which He realizes His victory in human hearts. This forgiveness then signifies that man is established in the new Covenant, it means that the bands of communion between God and man, which had been broken, are joined again. A new relation of confidence is established. It is all an action of the unmerited love of God, of the love that directs itself to the unworthy sinner. Forgiveness, remission of sins, is the way in which this new communion is being realized.

As regards this new relationship to God three things ought especially to be emphasized. First that—as has already been said—it is here a matter of real communion. It is perhaps not unnecessary to lay stress upon this fact—against metaphysical theories of a transcendentalism which suggest that the divine and the human, God and man, are and must be separated as long as history lasts. Secondly, justification is necessarily connected with a new life, *i.e.* with 'sanctification'; it includes 'sanctification'. The Christian life must, as long as it lasts, be a life of 'sanctification'. 'The old man must daily die to sin and the new man daily arise' (The Short Catechism of Luther). The Christian life is, and must be, a perpetual conflict against sin. It is a life that stands in the grace of God but at the same time is a life standing under His judgment. Therefore it cannot be that faith in salvation can get the character of *securitas*, of presumptuous security. Thirdly, the new relationship to God means that the life of man is placed at the service of God. There is no cleft between religion and ethics. They are joined in a unity. There is no reason to ask for any special ethical 'motifs'. What happens is that the love

of God takes man up into His communion and
so *sends him on His errands.* 'The love of Christ
constraineth us.'

The key word of the Reformation, 'justification
by faith alone' was indeed, if rightly understood,
a word out of the heart of Christian faith. But it
is easily misunderstood, not only by Churches
outside the Churches of the Reformation but also
within these Churches. Chiefly in two ways it
has been wrongly interpreted. First, it is misunderstood if you consider 'faith' as a condition
on the side of man for gaining the grace of God,
as an achievement of man that makes him worthy
of the divine love. So it has very often been interpreted, even in Protestant theology. But the real
meaning of the formula of the Reformation is
this: 'Justification by faith alone' means nothing
but justification through the love of God alone.
'Faith' means simply that the power, which
creates and decides the relationship of salvation,
is nothing but God's love. But then, if on this
account faith itself is here considered as a work
of God, the formula can easily be misunderstood
in quite the opposite way: it can be said that the
formula completely denies human activity and
so destroys human responsibility. Even if the
formula has often been interpreted in this way,
it is obvious that that does not correspond to the
intention of Luther. His books are full of utter-

ances that most strongly emphasize the claim on the human will and the responsibility of man. When he denounces 'justification through works of man', he does not deny the engagement of the will of man. It is rather a question of distinction between two different relationships to God, the relationship through works and the relationship by faith. The main thing is now that in the relationship of faith *all is stamped and decided by the love of God*. This relation to God is what it is through God's love which at the same time judges and saves. It is this power alone that overcomes and subdues man, that places him in the communion of love and constrains him to go its errands.

It could, I think, scarcely be denied that this view is fundamentally Christian and consonant with the revelation of God in Christ. If so, it is but an expression of the universal Christian message, and no special privilege for the Churches of the Reformation. It is obvious that it has not always been preserved in these Churches. It may be doubted if there are any Churches that have suffered so much as these Churches from the confusion between Christianity and the religiosity of self-glorification.

V. LOVE

All that the Christian faith has to say about the revelation of God is summed up in God's love: 'God is love.' Faith cannot say anything about God that is not a statement about His love. The Majesty of God is the Majesty of His love. The Righteousness of God is the Righteousness of His love. The Judgment of God is the Judgment of His love. God's love reveals itself in the actions of Incarnation, Resurrection and Justification. In the Incarnation love gives itself, for the sake of mankind it enters into the world of sin and death. In the Resurrection the way of sacrificial love leads to victory and to the building up of the Church of God. In Justification love realizes its victory in human hearts.

Now it cannot be denied that in the history of Christendom the love of God has often been interpreted in a very shallow way; and then it has lost its strength and majesty. This being the case, it is not surprising that there have been reactions on the part of theology, and that such reactions have sometimes tended to move love from the centre of Christian faith. But in truth the evil of a shallow interpretation of love cannot be cured by thoughts that confine love and that limit it by other 'qualities' in God, but only by seeing the love of God as it is revealed in the life and work of Christ, where it appears in its purity, in its radical and judging opposition against the powers of evil, and at the same time in all its depth as spontaneous and sacrificing love. Any theology that in any way conceals the truth that love is the centre and the all-dominating content of the revelation of God is from the Christian point of view a false theology, that obscures the revelation of God given to us in Christ.

When considering the relations between the Old and the New Covenant we have already paid attention to the two main features of the love of God as revealed in the work of Christ: God's love does not have its ground in any value of its object; it is spontaneous, free, overflowing, without limits, *gratia praeveniens*: and God's love gives itself for us, sacrifices itself and reveals its majesty in the way of sacrifice. It may here be added that these two features are reflected in the sacraments of Baptism and the Holy Eucharist. Baptism is the sacrament of *gratia praeveniens*; it is the action of the love of God that seeks us before we seek God, it tells us that this love of God is the only foundation upon which Christian faith and Christian life can build. The Holy Eucharist is the sacrament of suffering and victorious love. We here meet the love that goes the way of sacrifice unto death, that gives itself for us. But the Holy Eucharist is not only the sacrament of sacrifice. It is at the same time also the sacrament of victory. It is the sacrament in which the living Lord Himself is working in His Church and takes us into communion with Himself. Here we are looking into the depths of love. Nowhere is the heart of the revelation of God more deeply unveiled than in the Holy Eucharist. There Christian faith finds the revelation of God in its most concentrated form.

Christianity has but one commandment—the commandment of love. 'A new commandment I give unto you, that ye love one another; as I have loved you, that ye also love one another.' Christianity has but one gospel—the gospel of the love (ἀγάπη) of God as it is being revealed in the work of Christ. This love is at the same time the ground and the content of our faith. And it is likewise this love that separates Christianity from all the religions of the world and from all non-Christian theories of life. It is often said that nowadays a new heathenism is growing up within Christendom, and the fact cannot be denied. What is the note of this heathenism? It may appear in many forms, but the decisive thing about it is always that men are putting their confidence in something else than the love of God, or that they set limits to the exercise of love—limits of race, nationality and so forth; and that at the same time human self-glorification is in the ascendant. That means that Christianity is going out and heathenism is coming in.

In conclusion, two points must be mentioned— the immediacy of God's revelation and its unfathomableness.

The saving revelation of God meets us through historical means, viz. through the means of the Word and the sacraments. From the side of mysticism it is often said that the relation between God and man would not be a direct and immediate relation if mediated by means of history such as Word and sacraments; and for itself mysticism claims a more immediate relation to God. In such a statement, however, there is a fatal confusion of thought. First, this claim of mysticism must be denied. If mysticism is in fact based on a metaphysical speculation about immanence, and seeks God first of all in the depths of the human soul, there is no place at all for a real relation between God and man. The 'divine' that man can so find is only the supposed divinity of man. Secondly, the alternative, whether God works 'through means' *or* 'immediately' is a wrong and confused alternative. From the point of view of faith itself it does not exist. It disappears as soon as we consider God's activity in revelation. If God speaks to us and acts upon us through Word and sacraments, He speaks and acts always immediately and directly. Either we hear His voice speaking directly to us or we do not hear it at all.

As to the character of the revelation of God, the following position must be emphasized in conclusion: revelation unveils the essence, the heart of God, but at the same time it puts us before the unfathomable. God is at the same time the revealed and the hidden God, *Deus revelatus et Deus absconditus.*

Faith has no doubts as to the will and heart of God. That God is incarnate in Christ means that He is no more only the great Unknown. Faith *knows*. It has something quite definite to say about the will of God and His actions towards man. As regards the revelation of God in Christ, faith says: *such* is God, here we really find His will and His heart—there is no other God, there is only this God. He alone is the God of heaven and earth, the God of eternity.

But all that now has been said would be misleading if at the same time we did not consider that God is for faith also the Unfathomable and Inscrutable. It is precisely in the presence of the revelation of the will of God that faith must confess that His ways are fathomless and His judgments inscrutable. The God who reveals Himself is at the same time the hidden God, who dwells in light that none can approach, whom no man has ever seen or can see. Thereby the statements of faith are radically differentiated from every kind of rational and metaphysical speculation.

It is important to see in what way God appears to faith as the Unfathomable. It does not mean only that the revelation of God has certain limits. It does not mean only that, as long as we live under the conditions of this life, there are questions that cannot be answered and riddles that cannot be explained. It does not mean only that faith in God cannot be transformed into a rational explanation of the world, which would make the divine government of the world transparently clear. It means also that precisely the revelation of God itself has the character of unfathomableness. If the depth of the revelation of God is the love that gives itself for the sake of communion with sinful man, then this love itself is unfathomable, inscrutable. Thus God is for faith at the same time God the revealed and God the inscrutable. In fact, this rule is applicable for faith: the more fully God reveals Himself and faith looks into the secret of the divine heart, the more God appears as the Inscrutable. St. Paul has good reasons for speaking of himself as a minister of the mystery of God, of God's secret truths.

This paper has emphasized the love of God as the content of revelation. In the present state of the world this love is hidden. For at present we

find quite other forces predominating. In our time
the world is more than ever filled with hostility,
fear, anxiety and brutal lust of power. There is
little sign of the love that casts out fear. Strong
ideals are fighting against the Christian gospel.
Yet is it not at the same time true that the light of
love shines in the darkness and that the darkness
cannot master it? Is it not true that the light of
the love of God commends itself, as I venture to
say, more than ever to the world's conscience? Is
not the present state of the world crying out for
the spirit of love? What other power can give
us the help we so sorely need? If we look openly
and without illusion at the actual situation, and if
at the same time our eye has caught only a glint
of the light that proceeds from the love of God,
we can give only one answer—the answer returned
by Christ's disciples, 'Lord, to whom shall we go?
thou hast the words of eternal life. And we believe
and are sure that thou art that Christ, the Son
of the living God.'

INDEX

Index